Key Perspectives on Dyslexia

This indispensable text critically sets out the skills and knowledge required by a specialist educator for students who present with dyslexia. Key issues in the education and care of those affected by dyslexia are critically explained and explored, with the highly experienced authors showing how research can inform and enrich the ways in which an educator responds to these issues.

Chapters in this accessible text include:

- detailed case studies disclosing how dyslexia presents in different individuals and which richly illuminate the issues considered by each chapter;
- a concise examination of reading instruction in the context of typically developing students and in relation to those who present with dyslexia;
- guidance on how to identify possible dyslexia and key issues to consider in referral and assessment of those affected;
- consideration of intelligence and how this figures in relation to assessment for dyslexia;
- comprehensive evaluation of the role of behaviour in relation to dyslexia.

The British Dyslexia Association professional criteria provides an anchor throughout for this book's content, as chapters are explicitly mapped to their specific professional criteria and underpinned by this internationally recognised professional framework. *Key Perspectives on Dyslexia* is an essential text for educators and a landmark guide for educational practice and policy.

David Armstrong is Lecturer in Special and Inclusive Education at the University of South Australia, having previously worked in the UK as a specialist teacher and as a researcher.

Garry Squires is Director of the Doctorate in Educational Psychology programme at the University of Manchester, UK.

Key Perspectives on Dyslexia

An essential text for educators

David Armstrong and
Garry Squires

Routledge
Taylor & Francis Grou

LONDON AND NEW YOR

First published 2015
by Routledge
2 Park Square, Milton Park, Abingdon, Oxon OX14 4RN

and by Routledge
711 Third Avenue, New York, NY 10017

Routledge is an imprint of the Taylor & Francis Group, an informa business

British Library Cataloguing in Publication Data
A catalogue record for this book is available from the British Library

Library of Congress Cataloging-in-Publication Data
Armstrong, David.
Key perspectives on dyslexia : an essential text for educators / David Armstrong, Garry Squires.
pages cm
1. Dyslexic children–Education. 2. Learning disabled children–Education.
3. Reading–Remedial teaching. 4. Reading disability 5. Learning disabilities.
I. Squires, Garry. II. Title.
LC4708.A76 2014
371.9–dc23
2014010455

ISBN: 978-0-415-81987-9 (hbk)
ISBN: 978-0-415-81988-6 (pbk)
ISBN: 978-1-315-75636-3 (ebk)

Typeset in Sabon
by Deer Park Productions

Contents

Illustrations

Figures

Tables

About the authors

Dr David Armstrong

David is currently Lecturer in Special Education and Inclusion at the University of South Australia. From 2008 to 2011 he was a senior lecturer for the MA in Education (Special Educational Needs and Disability and Inclusion) at Edge Hill University, UK. In 2010 he led a major UK-based initiative on teacher workforce development. This was about extending the number of qualified specialist educators for students with dyslexia, following professional guidelines set out by the British Dyslexia Association (BDA) and as a result of recommendations by Sir Jim Rose (2009). This book had its origins in this initiative. From 1996 to 2008 he worked in the UK as a specialist teacher with a range of children and young people with disabilities and barriers to learning, including the homeless, excluded children and adults with learning disabilities. During this time he assessed and supported numerous children, young people and adults presenting with dyslexia.

He is author of a range of publications including: Armstrong and Squires (eds) (2012) *Contemporary Issues in Special Educational Needs*, Maidenhead: Open University Press/McGraw-Hill Education; and Armstrong *et al.* (2015) *Understanding Behaviour: Research and Practice for Teachers*, Cambridge: Cambridge University Press. David is an active graduate member of the British Psychological Society (BPS).

Dr Garry Squires

Garry is currently the Director of the Doctorate in Educational Psychology programme at the University of Manchester, UK. He completed his training as an educational psychologist in 1996 and has worked in the field of dyslexia and special educational needs. He is a Fellow of the British Psychological Society and Registered Practitioner Educational Psychologist as well as being an academic and researcher. His first book (2003, with Sally McKeown) *Supporting Children with Dyslexia*, London: Continuum, focused on the way in which teachers can practically support children and it complements this book, which focuses on understanding why educators approach dyslexia in the way that they do.

Acknowledgements

David Armstrong

To my wife Gill: what use are books without a life filled with love?

Garry Squires

To Louise, who has a passion to improve the lives of all those she encounters, especially mine.

Introduction

This book is, in part, a response to the question of what skills, knowledge and attributes are required by a specialist educator for children or young people who present with dyslexia. Our original brief was to address the various facets of this professional role and as set out by the British Dyslexia Association (BDA) in their criteria for courses leading to Approved Teacher Status and associate membership of the BDA (BDA, 2012). A major educational review in the UK by Sir Jim Rose (2009) was the policy driver for this framework, suggesting the need for many more specialist teachers with these specific skills and knowledge to support students presenting in schools with dyslexia.

While developing this book, however, it soon became apparent that there is increasing momentum across the English-speaking world, and in important emerging nations such as China, for a specialist educator whose practice is focused in helping children who struggle with reading, writing and other essential ingredients of effective academic study. The Australian Federal Government has, for example, signalled a recent policy shift towards recognising dyslexia as a discrete entity (Australian Government, 2013). This potentially heralds a major change in a range of areas across Australian states including, for example, the establishment of dyslexia-friendly schools, plus specialist educators who lead assessment and/or support for children with dyslexia (Australian Government, 2013). In light of such developments, we wanted our book to be international in perspective and offer support to such national policy initiatives, with their increasingly global ripples of influence.

Sharing our experiences of the reality of practice in this field with readers is also an important aim of this publication. As specialist practitioners, we seek, in what follows, to set out some of the key issues for educational practice from our perspective having, collectively, assessed/supported hundreds of students with dyslexia over the years. In light of this, we also suggest that, while helpful, professional criteria from the BDA are only a conceptual guide and that the usefulness of criteria can only be continually judged by how relevant these are in the setting. Flexible application of professional criteria is particularly important for international readers located in, for example, the US, Canada and China: how these are applied here will, to a significant extent, be dependent on unique local systems, traditions and customs, including whether English (or another language) is the primary medium of instruction. Furthermore, it becomes apparent that there are different viewpoints and agendas at play when considering dyslexia and this pulls the educator in many different directions. Professional judgements designed to guide practice are important in deciding how best to operate in local conditions. One of our aims has been to present these tensions around key perspectives surrounding the politics and social construction of dyslexia.

In this spirit, we have been selective in the focus of chapters, choosing what we consider the key issues for a specialist teacher to understand and respond to. In our approach we also kept the original BDA criteria, to some extent, as specific anchor point: what follows, for example, addresses how psychometric tests are used and understood – a key component in the BDA criteria for Approved Teacher Status. This topic is addressed in Chapter 2 and in Chapter 5.

We suggest that this book sets itself within a wider perspective by adopting this approach and by honestly presenting some of the real-world complexity of these contested issues. This underpins the critical question that specific chapters address and which, we think, are of great relevance to a specialist educator in actual practice. These are reflected in the content of chapters:

- How should we conceive of dyslexia as an observable phenomenon (Chapter 1)?
- How should we approach teaching reading to individuals who have struggled to learn to read and who present with dyslexia (Chapter 2)?
- What principles should guide assessment for dyslexia (Chapter 3)?
- What role does behaviour play in supporting students with dyslexia (Chapter 4)?
- Should intelligence tests be used in assessment for dyslexia and if so for what purpose (Chapter 5)?
- Are the issues surrounding dyslexia any different in higher education than in school-based education (Chapter 6)?

As in other publications we have authored (Armstrong and Squires, 2012), we encourage you to have a sceptical, questioning view on the issues for research, practice and policy which we outline in what follows. It should also be noted that while our views as authors converge on many issues in this field, we do not always absolutely agree on every issue. For example we have different, but not opposing view on the merits of IQ (Intelligence Quotient) testing, which is discussed in Chapter 5 and also Chapter 2. As researchers and scholars, we think that this is absolutely fine. In fact, we suggest that informed debate and the constant testing out of accepted ideas and practices (including our own) is profoundly useful for intellectual progress and for the positive evolution of practice. We also recommend being open to change as helpful to your own professional role as a specialist educator. We encourage you to reflect on each of the issues and to decide where you stand on each one; you will find reflective question boxes dotted throughout each chapter.

To clarify an important point, while this book is rooted in our real-world experiences as practitioners, it is not an explicit 'how to' practical/ 'teachers tips' guide to practice with individuals who appear to have dyslexia. In fact, we doubt that the latter would actually be useful for the reader in the absence of an understanding of the complex issues around dyslexia, which can only become apparent through *significant practical experience* in a setting with learners affected by this complex phenomenon. Such experience will offer insight into how to effectively support learners' progress. Our focus is not so much on the 'how to' but on the 'why we should'. Having said that, you will find more general pointers in the text about 'how' to deal with the 'why'.

The purpose of this book is to scaffold your experience and draw detailed, research-supported attention to the wider issues or more difficult questions which arise along the way. We hope that it provides, therefore, a thought-provoking, helpful and informative guide for your journey to a fuller understanding.

Psychology, education and dyslexia

One important quality of dyslexia as a space for research and scholarly enquiry is that it spans psychology (in all its sub-disciplines) as much as it does education. In fact, study of individuals who present with dyslexia has been a rich and important vein of insight into the genetic, cognitive and neuroanatomical/neuropsychological dimensions of language acquisition, language development and language use (Heim and Grande, 2012; Vellutino *et al.*, 2004). Other areas – for example, disability studies (Riddick, 2001) – and also disciplines – for example, psychiatry – have also made important contributions in understanding how dyslexia is experienced by those affected and its connections to their health and wider welfare (Levy *et al.*, 2012).

One challenge which emerges from this exciting interdisciplinary richness is that the specialist educator is overwhelmed in a sea of research calling on language and concepts from different disciplines or sub-disciplines. In addition, as with other areas of academic enquiry, many of the research papers potentially available address a very specialist audience, using specific concepts and technical language. In many cases, research publically available about dyslexia presupposes that the reader is a postgraduate student or established scholar. Many educators who are new to this area and have not (or not recently, at least) studied beyond an undergraduate degree report that they feel overwhelmed by the sheer variety and complexity of scholarly research around dyslexia.

It might, therefore, be useful at this point to consider the descriptions below of the range of disciplines and sub-disciplines and how they approach the category of dyslexia, explaining some of the many ways in which researchers have examined the subject from different perspectives over the last 30 years. The name of the discipline is given in bold; some examples of the type/typical focus of studies associated with that discipline in reference to dyslexia are given.

Genetic/biology: epidemiological (whole population)-based studies; familial incidence (do family members of those affected also show signs of dyslexia?); genetic markers for dyslexia in affected individuals; dyslexia and gender.

Neuropsychology: role of specific brain areas in dyslexia/presentation of dyslexia (neuroanatomy); brain function/brain structure and reading; role of auditory or of visual processing systems in dyslexia; eye-tracking; EEG and fMRI studies brain function in those with dyslexia; acquired disabilities affecting reading (such as injuries due to a road traffic accident [RTA] or head trauma of another cause).

Psychology: cognition as an information processing model with cognitive factors affecting dyslexia; co-morbidity or co-occurrence (e.g. attention deficit hyperactivity disorder and dyslexia); use of psychometric testing; relationships between working memory and dyslexia; dyslexia and phonological processing (how sounds are processed); dyslexia and mental health; relationships between dyslexia and other language disorders, such as specific language impairment (SLI); dyslexia and behavioural factors.

Educational psychology: aspects of practice by educational or school psychologists in directly supporting those affected; educational policy; applied psychological theory relating to dyslexia; evaluation of interventions with those affected; use of psychometric testing in a school or educational context for dyslexia; educator practice (from a psychological perspective) and multidisciplinary (educator–psychologist) practice to support those affected; dyslexia and behavioural factors/issues; the role for educational psychologists (EPs) in supporting educators in their professional learning and practice around dyslexia.

Education: educational practice, educational evaluation or policy pertaining to dyslexia: inclusion; behaviour and dyslexia; educational policy; professional roles in supporting children with dyslexia; literacy and dyslexia; evaluation of interventions; teaching reading/reading instruction and dyslexia; spelling/writing and dyslexia; mathematics and dyslexia (factors in teaching mathematics [or math] to students with dyslexia); dyslexia and behaviour.

Sociology of education: dyslexia and disability (disability studies); social and educational inclusion and dyslexia; dyslexia and identity; dyslexia and relationships (particularly with a student's educators and with their family); dyslexia and criminality/deviance (including studies of the possible prevalence of dyslexia in the prison population); dyslexia and gender.

As might be gathered, there is considerable overlap and replication where issues affecting learners are examined from different disciplinary perspectives. One aim of this book is to help the specialist educator make sense of these many different perspectives, therefore avoiding the overload sometimes provoked by even a brief survey of this complex area. In presenting these closely together, it becomes apparent that the disciplines do not always fit well together. Theories which seek to explain the underlying cause and presentation or 'symptoms' of dyslexia are the focus for concise discussion in Chapter 1, 'What is dyslexia?' Yet these are presented alongside some of the ways in which society creates the disability of dyslexia.

We also, however, present selected findings from research in the context of the key practical issues we think you are likely to experience in your setting. Supporting students who present with dyslexia in terms of their reading (Chapter 2) and also in terms of their behaviour (Chapter 4) is often at the forefront of the mind of specialist teachers in daily practice. 'Reading' and 'behaviour' are, however, controversial and often politically charged areas for educational practice and education policy (see, respectively, Chapter 2 and Chapter 4 for further discussion); they provoke considerable debate among educational professionals and policy-makers. In concert with the sheer diversity of research about dyslexia, such confused and confusing debates can present a lack of clarity for educators about their choices in and around practice.

Stanovich (2000), who has historically been an important researcher in the field of how typically developing children learn to read and also in terms of understanding dyslexia, suggests that opposition between 'whole language advocates' and 'proponents of decoding skills' has been an unhelpful 'confusing mix of science and politics' for educators (p. 361). He adds: 'fortunately, the best teachers have often been wise enough to incorporate the most effective practices from the two different approaches into their instructional programmes' (p. 361). We would agree with this observation: 'what works' for an individual affected by dyslexia in terms of progressing their reading and what works for the educator teaching them will often differ from case to case and should not, therefore, be generalised into a 'one size fits all' framework of any kind.

As we highlight in Chapter 2, practitioners should feel entirely confident to select, use and evaluate/test a range of strategies to support a student's reading. This recommendation also applies to developing a student's writing (consisting of the sub-topics of a learner's handwriting, their written vocabulary, their use of grammar and level of compositional skills). A high-quality, carefully considered and carefully supported diagnostic assessment of a student is the best vehicle for designing focused, responsive and informed support for a student with dyslexia and in guiding what mix of strategies might be most effective in each case. Issues to consider in gathering the data for a diagnostic assessment; in interpreting what this data means; and in communicating its implication to those directly affected, their family and other professionals are discussed in Chapter 3.

Indeed, using this (applied research case study) approach is arguably far more 'scientific' than inflexibly adopting a particular strategy because it is the latest recommendation by local or national policy. As we point out, there are fundamental unresolved scientific questions about how 'typically developing' children learn to read and a lack of clarity over to what extent or even *if* this complex process applies to individuals with dyslexia. We therefore urge a sceptical response towards any claim (by policy-makers, commercial organisations or the media) that there is an established evidence-base for particular practices (such as synthetic phonics) or that validates specific commercial products.

One progressive component of the BDA professional criteria is that they acknowledge the wider impact that difficulty with study and learning often has on the behaviour and welfare of those affected. They specify that a specialist educator should 'Demonstrate an understanding of the social, emotional and behavioural difficulties pupils with specific learning difficulties may encounter' (BDA, 2012, p. 3). It should be noted that this emphasis upon the personal, psychological difficulties often faced by children and young people in their education and who present with dyslexia has a strong basis in research (Armstrong and Humphrey, 2009; Riddick, 2010). We would also suggest, in light of our own experience, that these difficulties are an important factor that specialist educators should take into account in everyday practice: our goal is to mitigate their severity and ensure that, so far as is possible, they minimally affect the academic progress of individuals.

These concerns around behaviour in the context of dyslexia are the focus for Chapter 4. On a pragmatic level, the negative emotions aroused by difficult or even traumatic experiences for those affected by dyslexia can, in some cases, have a negative, overshadowing effect on all of their time in a setting, with spin offs in withdrawn (disengaged) and/or externalising (challenging, disruptive) behaviours. For educators, the immediate priority in such cases is to re-engage the student as a priority and seek support from their immediate colleagues, external agencies and/or the student's family.

Chapter 4 discusses these challenges in detail. It also explores some of the wider factors around any consideration of behaviour in the context of supporting students who present with dyslexia but who might also have other co-existing conditions such as social emotional and behavioural difficulties (SEBD) – offering insight into how they can complicate efforts to support those affected. Functional behaviour analysis (FBA) is outlined and suggested as one useful framework for a specialist educator to call upon in this context, particularly if used with the support of an educational psychologist, school psychologist or other allied professional with a background in the use of FBA (Cooper, 2011).

Three case studies

As you read this book, we want you to be thinking critically about the issues that are presented and to think about the implications for dyslexic learners. What follows are three case studies of children and young people who present, in quite different ways, with a learning profile indicative of dyslexia. These are drawn from our experience of real individuals and are an amalgam of real children or young people, significantly changed to prevent any recognition of an individual. We thought it worthwhile to present cases with some level of authenticity and to provoke the readers' critical consideration in light of their own experiences of children who are described as dyslexic.

Wherever possible we have attempted to adjust each case to be general enough to fit in any locality across the English-speaking world, but specific enough to convey its fine grain. Those readers interested in the broad perspectives of research in this area might consider how case study methodology has a strong tradition in research conducted in educational settings with children who have disability (Cohen *et al.*, 2007; Yin, 2014)

Each case presented also underpins one or more issues which this book considers – such as, the role of behaviour in considering practice with children who present with dyslexia addressed by Chapter 4; or how to teach reading to those affected, which is the main focus of Chapter 2. One of the advantages of case studies is that they allow a deeper appreciation of wider issues for practice without losing the often unique way in which disability can affect children and young people (Armstrong, 2013; Cohen *et al.*, 2007).

In reading what follows, we suggest that you to compare and contrast each case: are there any differences or similarities? To help prompt this process of critical consideration we have added a set of reflective questions at the end of each case.

John's story

Age: 14 years
Gender: male
Profile: typically affected by dyslexia, at risk of academic failure, motivated but at risk of developing emotional difficulties associated with dyslexia

John attends a mainstream high school located in the suburbs of a medium-sized city. He has no visible disability and appears typically developing with good social skills. His demeanour changes when we ask him about his reading and writing: we can sense that he has spoken to many other professionals about this issue throughout his life already and there is a hint of sadness in his voice. John reports that his problems with reading and writing started once at primary school, aged five years old: 'I didn't learn to read like the others in my class and my teacher couldn't understand why.' He reports that he had additional help with reading and with writing at primary school and at home. It is significant that John's teachers at primary school (eventually) acknowledged that his significant lack of attainment in reading and writing was not due to lack of intelligence or application: 'At first they thought that my problems with reading and writing were because I would not try hard enough, then they started to notice that I seemed to learn differently: the special teacher noticed this and sent me for tests,' he adds 'these showed that I am dyslexic.' John also reports a troubled period in his academic life before his study difficulties were accommodated by the school. 'I started to hate school: just seeing everybody else getting better at reading and writing and there I was stuck on the baby books. I simply ran out of school a few times, just to get away from how hard it was. The teachers and my parents went crazy when I did that.' It was only after these events that an assessment by a qualified psychologist was carried out, which John's parents funded.

He also reports having had extra parental help at home during his early and primary/elementary education. As a person, John appears motivated but often also conveys frustration at the sheer effort he has to expend to make very modest progress in his reading, writing, spelling and related academic tasks. If we were to observe John 'on task' we would note that he often has subtle attentional difficulties and often has to 'self-talk' or prompt himself to remember what he is supposed to be doing – this is a learned behaviour which John has adopted and which is moderately successful.

A specialist screening by a speech and language professional would identify that John has a range of subtle difficulties in his expressive oral (spoken) language. This would include a pattern of difficulties in verbal articulation where John was 'stumbling' over words, with miscues and a pattern of spoonerisms/errors. Such miscues and spoonerisms are caused for John by fine-motor difficulties within the larynx and palate/and or disruption of phoneme retrieval and articulation. John can become 'tongue tied' and sounds in his spoken words (oral language) are noticeably 'mixed up' on some occasions – particularly when he is tired, anxious or excited. If we asked John to read aloud a short passage of text (a request which, even if carried out in private, would cause John some anxiety) then we would note that:

- His reading vocal tone was laborious and uncertain.
- He would perform significantly below age-related expectations.
- He would make frequent errors, particularly, in terms of handling the sound components in words, which are described as 'phonemes'.
- If we explored his understanding or comprehension of what he had read, we would find that he does not assimilate much of the basic content of what he reads – John is often so anxious about his reading and has to work so hard on his letter decoding that his comprehension is affected – see Chapter 2 of this book for further discussion about teaching reading to students with dyslexia.

If we were to test John's reading of single words with the kind of psychometric test used by a psychologist, he would probably perform, depending on the kind of day he is having, on or below the fifth percentile, with a standard score of 75. This is below the threshold prompting investigation of a standard score of 85 (85 is one standard deviation below the mean of 100) – see Chapter 3 in this book for further explanation – and would mean that 95 per cent of his peers would achieve at or above this level.

John's skills at writing are very weak indeed, as disclosed by careful analysis of a piece of written work which he was asked to complete for his English Composition coursework. If we were to test John's spelling on a single-word spelling test, we would find that it is even weaker than his reading in terms of what we might expect of a young person of his age, with him scoring in the third percentile, achieving a standard score of 72.

Many but not all of his educators at the high school he attends are supportive: some educators who teach John privately suggest that 'dyslexia doesn't exist' and doubt that John's problems are genuine. The school has a public commitment to full inclusion for students who are disabled and to 'meeting the varied needs of a diverse community' (high school website). One of John's parents reports similar academic difficulties at middle and high school and, although a highly successful adult with a small local business, reports 'giving up' on academic study aged 14. John is officially described as 'at risk' of academic failure.

John reports that he finds English particularly difficult at high school but that he enjoys and performs well at what adults have described as 'practical' subjects, including music and design technology. His teachers are worried that he will be unable to perform well in his final examinations at high school because his literacy is well below expected standards. John receives one-to-one support for his reading and spelling in the classroom from a classroom assistant/school services officer (SSO) or student support officer. Support for John's reading, for example, is focused on helping John improve his reading fluency, word recognition (sight vocabulary) and comprehension, with some intensive instruction done in private.

If we were to ask John about his memory he would self-report that he is often characterised by others as 'forgetful'; if we were to test John's working memory – for example, using a digit span test – we would find that he is significantly below age-expected norms/where we might expect him to be. John's mum, who has been very supportive of his learning, often helps him to remember things he needs for school, using prompts and self-organisational strategies.

John tries to be positive about his future and would like to set up his own business, like his father, post-high school. Several of John's educators are, however, less positive given the extent of his problems with study, with reading and with writing, but they recognise that he is a committed and generally motivated student. His music teacher particular praises the steady progress being made by John in both his music theory and music practice elements of study.

Reflective questions

What strengths does John have? How can these be used to motivate him?
What are John's main challenges for progress with study and learning?
What should be the focus for supporting John's learning?
How vulnerable is John to educational non-achievement?
How vulnerable is John to educational failure due to poor behaviour, educational exclusion or truancy/drop out?
What role does the attitude of teachers potentially play in the success or otherwise of support/programmes/interventions designed to help John?
What caught your interest about this case/what do you regard as significant?

Ahmed's story

Age: 18 years
Gender: male
Profile: atypically affected by dyslexia, at major risk of academic failure, with co-occurring disabilities/SEBD

Ahmed is an engaging young man who has recently moved to the area with his family and has started to attend his local college for further/post-high school study. He is friendly and sociable and hails from a locally respected, devoutly religious family – Ahmed does community work for a local charity outside of study. His educator has referred him to the college inclusive education assessment team/learning support team for a thorough assessment as it has been noted that Ahmed has a variety of difficulties with academic study. Because of these problems with study, the word 'dyslexia' has been mentioned by educators in connection with Ahmed, but no information is available – such as a report by a school psychologist or educational psychologist; this is because his parents have moved across the country/interstate several times.

Ahmed also speaks fluent Farsi, a language spoken in Iran and neighbouring countries. His parents, who emigrated from Iran many years ago, are actually very worried about Ahmed's future and have noticed the same difficulties which prompted his tutor to refer him.

His tutor was, initially, concerned about the standard of Ahmed's reading and writing. If we tested this using an age-matched text as part of a good-quality, holistic, diagnostic assessment we would discover that Ahmed reads confidently, but can understand little of what he has read; he can decode very effectively in written English, but his comprehension is very weak. This is only apparent after:

1 informing Ahmed that we will be asking him some questions about what he is about to read;
2 asking Ahmed to read an age-appropriate passage of text aloud; and
3 asking Ahmed a set of questions about the passage, starting by posing general questions, such as 'What was that about?', and becoming steadily more specific: 'What happened when ...?'

When you meet Ahmed to discuss these issues he cheerily reports that he wants you to 'look into his head' and cure him and that he is enjoying college. His odd/unusual phrasing and immature oral language might seem concerning. If we were to observe Ahmed in class, over time, we would note a deteriorating level of attention and gradually diminishing understanding of what the educator is asking him to do, alongside significant weaknesses in his reading comprehension. We would also note the deterioration in the quality and quantity of his social relationships with increasing isolation for Ahmed. After assessment, a speech and language professional would note a longstanding weakness in his receptive language ability – in his understanding of the detail of what others say to him.

Testing Ahmed using standardised assessments for his reading, writing and spelling (often spelling is tested as a proxy for writing) would suggest that he has major problems with reading comprehension, spelling and handwriting. The precise extent of this underachievement is, however, unclear because his performance varies significantly and from hour to hour. Test scores are, at best, a snapshot and there is a fundamental ethical issue of consent to consider about conducting tests with him when it becomes clear that Ahmed does not understand many events around him.

After gaining further qualifications at college Ahmed would like to train to become a doctor, but his family are, day by day, becoming so concerned about his wellbeing that they are considering asking him to withdraw from study at the local college. His difficulties with literacy and with academic study are, in some respects, the least pressing issues for Ahmed, his educators and his family.

If we were to take Ahmed to a medical or health professional they would refer him, depending upon location, for specialist assessment by a psychiatrist, a specialist disability clinical team or the Child and Adolescent Mental Health Service (CAMHS). They would discover that Ahmed has, for several years, struggled with the effects of a learning disability which, to some extent, presents as dyslexia but which is now co-occurring with SEBD, bordering on meeting the criteria for a mental health problem. Ahmed and his family require support from a team of professionals, including educators where Ahmed studies, to ensure that he has the best chance for a positive future.

Reflective questions

What strengths does Ahmed have? How can these be used to support him?

What are Ahmed's main challenges for progress with study and learning? Are they actually on account of him having dyslexia? Are they even actually to do with his education or wider health and wellbeing?

What role does deteriorating attention have in Ahmed's study difficulties?

What should be the focus for supporting Ahmed's learning?

What caught your interest about this case/what do you regard as significant?

Lara's story

Age: 10 years
Gender: female
Profile: less severely affected by dyslexia, self-remediated, with high levels of motivation – resilient

Lara, despite facing significant challenges in her learning, is determined and motivated to do well academically. Lara is a socially popular student who studies at a school which is combined primary/elementary and middle. The school has a strong local reputation for its commitment to children's growth in the widest sense – personal, social, intellectual and also academic. Lara also receives one-to-one tuition after school, which is focused on improving Lara's reading, writing, spelling and study organisation. Lara is already looking forward to high school and training to be a fashion designer afterwards. Art and design are personal interests for Lara, who excels in these areas of the curriculum.

One distinguishing emotional feature of Lara is that she is has reacted to the notion that she 'has dyslexia' in a positive, adaptive way. If we asked her what 'having dyslexia' means for her, she would say 'trying harder with my reading, spelling, writing and study', evoking Lara's resilience to the challenges which she faces with schoolwork. This quality has also been carried through into the way in which Lara engages enthusiastically with support for her learning at school and at home. Lara comes from a one-parent family and lives with her mum – who is a dentist at a local dental practice. Lara's mum is highly supportive, but incredibly busy.

Lara's reading, writing, spelling and study are affected by dyslexia in a manner which is less severe than many children with dyslexia: this is at least partly because Lara has self-remediated some of the problems with learning to read, write and study and is constantly seeking routes around academic problems she encounters. Because of this, if we tested Lara's reading on a single-word, standardised reading test, we would find that she achieves at the 16th percentile, with a standard score of 85: this is exactly on the threshold/borderline to prompt investigation. It is important to note, however, that the precise figures for Lara's performance on reading, spelling and writing are not wholly indicative of Lara's case: they do not tell the full story.

If we listened to Lara reading an age-appropriate passage of text aloud we would hear that Lara makes a significant number of errors, particularly in terms of reading longer multisyllabic words and also in terms of hesitancy/difficulty around her approach to words (word-attack). In general, Lara's reading is significantly slower than we might expect and slower than that of her non-dyslexic peers. Lara requires significantly more time to process written text and makes a small but significant number of errors in processing: her decoding of phonetically regular words is far less affected by problems than her decoding of phonetically irregular words – words which cannot be 'sounded out' in written English (see Chapter 2). Despite these difficulties, Lara has adequate comprehension of what she reads and can grasp its main features – although this is often achieved by having to reread text several times.

Lara's progress in her reading has been gained through sheer effort since she was aged six and early problems with literacy were first noted. When Lara was aged eight and a half years old, her mother paid privately for a full diagnostic assessment by a local psychologist. The psychologist's report suggested that Lara 'presents with a pattern of cognitive difficulties consistent with the specific learning difficulty, dyslexia'. The report also noted that Lara 'appeared to perform poorly in tasks involving working memory' and also noted that she presented difficulties with 'numeric sequencing' (sequencing numbers).

Despite the fact that dyslexia was not legally recognised by the local education authority/state education authority, Lara's primary/elementary school accepted the findings of the psychologist's report, unofficially at least, and had already put in place strong support for Lara by the time she was aged seven. A local small charity, Dyslexia Ahead, supported Lara's mum in her efforts and advocated on her behalf at the school. Dyslexia Ahead also helped to arrange for the one-to-one tuition which Lara receives after school.

One of the major problems which Lara faces is with her understanding and application of mathematics. If we asked her to describe what happens when she works on numbers Lara would describe how she 'gets mixed up and forgets' basic mathematical operations and calculations. If we observed Lara's work in mathematics we would note that she presents anxious behaviour when confronted with tasks in this area of the curriculum: Lara highlights how she 'gets flustered' and forgets where she is with sequences of numbers. Lara also often misreads or omits decimal points, loses place value and reports problems with directional value. For example, when presented with the number '6102', Lara writes this as '612' or 2061; when asked to work out $5 - 10$, Lara calculates $5 - 1$ or attempts $10 \div 5$. On many occasions, Lara simply uses avoidant behaviour when faced with tasks from this important area of the curriculum. Those who educate Lara, and her mum, acknowledge that Lara faces significant challenges in this area. If we were to test Lara's performance in mathematics we would note that it is severely affected by anxiety. This means that any scores gained are probably not actually indicative of ability anyway, and that gleaning this information carries inherent ethical problems. Were we to test Lara, however, we would discover that she performs with a standard score of 78 and in the seventh percentile in mathematics for a child of her age.

Despite underlying problems with aspects of study, Lara is confident about her future at high school and beyond. In this Lara is typical of many, although significantly not all, children with dyslexia, who respond resiliently to the challenges it can pose for their study and wider life.

Reflective questions

What are Lara's main strengths? How has Lara's personal resilience contributed to her coping?

What, if any, impact has the attitude of the school and its educators/staff had in this case?

What remedial/coping strategies might Lara use to help with her reading, spelling and study?

Is Lara's performance wholly indicative of the extent of her underlying difficulties and, if not, why?

Is Lara likely to have educationally positive outcomes and, if so, why?

What are Lara's main challenges for effective study?

What should be the focus for supporting Lara's learning?

What caught your interest about this case/what do you regard as significant?

How this book maps to the BDA professional criteria for courses leading to Approved Teacher Status and associate membership of the BDA

In this book we broadly refer to the BDA professional criteria (BDA, 2012) as a framework for thinking about the skills, knowledge and attributes of a specialist teacher with students who present with dyslexia. No one book could, however, comprehensively cover every point from these criteria for every situation, given that how these are approached in part depends upon the context of practice – for example, whether in practice with young children or with adults; in a school or other setting; with students who already have been formally assessed and identified as having dyslexia or otherwise. Our aim has been to present information in a way which asks you to critically reflect on the issues presented.

International contexts

This book is also designed to be of value to educators across the English-speaking world and in other emerging nations such as, for example, China and India: any professional criteria in these many national contexts requires adaption to local needs and cultural interpretation. We suggest that readers carefully consider how the issues we highlight in this book and the following BDA professional criteria might apply to their particular context.

We hope, however, that mapping the BDA professional criteria to this book is helpful and that together they disclose an international framework for thinking about what a specialist educator understands and does in their daily practice. This can only be beneficial, we suggest, to affected students and all those involved in their education.

Criteria not covered

Several criteria which we have intentionally not included in what follows are best addressed, we think, by a professional update in the readers' own setting and in light of what is available at that time. These criteria, specifically, are:

1.7 The contribution of ICT in the screening and teaching of specific learning difficulties/dyslexia and a knowledge of relevant technical aids.

5.6 Understand and critically appraise the role of ICT in:
    5.6.1   the screening for and teaching of specific learning difficulties/ dyslexia
    5.6.2   the range of technical aids for teaching, writing and numeracy
    5.6.3   support and access to learning.

Table 0.1 BDA professional criteria and this book

BDA professional criteria	Relevant chapter or section in this book
Approved Teacher Status (ATS) and Approved Practitioner Status	
Core element	
Demonstrate an understanding of:	
1.1 the nature of dyslexia	Introduction, Chapter 1
1.2 good practice in Wave 1 teaching of literacy. This should include understanding of appropriate systematic phonics teaching programmes and the reading models on which interventions are based	Chapter 2, Conclusion
1.3 contemporary theories of the typical development of language, literacy and numeracy skills and how dyslexic learners may differ from those who are not experiencing difficulties in acquiring these skills	Introduction (case studies), Chapter 1, Chapter 2
1.4 principles underlying structured, sequential, multisensory teaching	Chapter 2, Chapter 3, Chapter 4, Conclusion
1.5 design and delivery of individual teaching programmes	Introduction, Chapter 2, Chapter 3, Chapter 4, Chapter 5
1.6 learning environment organisation facilitating individual learning	Introduction, Chapter 3, Chapter 4
1.8 methods and principles of staff development for an inclusive curriculum	Chapter 4, Chapter 6, Conclusion
Specialist element	
Demonstrate an ability to:	
2.1 identify learners with specific learning difficulties in the classroom	Chapter 3
2.2 make a diagnostic appraisal based on observation, assessment of attainments and the reports of other professionals	Chapter 3, Chapter 5
2.4 construct and evaluate a structured, sequential, multisensory teaching programme to meet specific individual needs at a basic level in learning	Introduction, Chapter 2, Chapter 3, Chapter 4, Chapter 5

(continued)

Table 0.1 BDA professional criteria and this book (Continued)

BDA professional criteria	Relevant chapter or section in this book
2.5 communicate effectively with teachers, parents and other professionals by verbal and written reports on the needs and achievements of learners with dyslexia	Introduction, Chapter 3
2.6 understand how to develop effective study methods, organisation skills and improved motivation and self-esteem for learners	Chapter 3, Chapter 4
2.7 model teaching and learning approaches and coach staff in their own and other schools	Introduction, Chapter 6, Conclusion

Table 0.2 Associate membership of the BDA and this book

Associate membership of the BDA (AMBDA) (postgraduate level)	
5 Core elements	
Understand and critically appraise:	
5.1.1 current research in specific learning difficulties/ dyslexia and its relevance for teaching learning	Introduction, Chapter 2, Chapter 5, throughout
5.1.2 theory and practice of psychometrics	Chapter 3, Chapter 5
5.1.3 relationship of that theory to the assessment of cognitive abilities and difficulties of pupils and students	Chapter 5, Chapter 3
5.2 competent preparation and dissemination of technical reports to specialist teachers and other professionals and non-professionals concerned with the support of students, including the provision of advice and recommendations to meet specific purposes	Chapter 3, Chapter 5
5.3 a range of learning strategies and structured, sequential, multisensory language and numeracy teaching programmes	Chapter 2, Chapter 3, Chapter 4
5.4 familiarity with the evidence-base concerning effective interventions for learners with dyslexia and literacy difficulties, and show how such knowledge may be used in monitoring and evaluating programmes of support	Introduction, Chapter 2
5.5 understanding of the implications of social, emotional, behavioural and community issues for dyslexic learners and their families. It is important that these issues are considered across the full age range so that current difficulties can be understood in relation either to their possible derivation or future implications	Chapter 3, Chapter 4, throughout

6 Specialist elements	
6.1 Develop and demonstrate the necessary knowledge and skills competently to observe diagnostically and assess the cognitive abilities and difficulties of pupils who fail to become competent in literacy and/or numeracy, and report appropriately on their needs and provision required	Chapter 3, Chapter 5
6. 2 Design, produce, deliver and critically evaluate appropriate programmes in relation to the assessed needs of a range of dyslexic pupils, making reference to current theory and research	Chapter 2, Chapter 3, Chapter 4
6.3 Demonstrate an understanding of the legal and professional issues that affect dyslexic pupils	Introduction, Chapter 6

Chapter 1

What is dyslexia?

What is dyslexia? This may seem like a question that should be easy to answer, given that we have been talking about dyslexia since it was first written about by Pringle Morgan in 1896 (Squires and McKeown, 2003, 2006). We should be able to give a clear description by now and start our book with a good understanding of the phenomenon that we are talking about. However, this is not the case. The term is open to debate and means many things to many people. Understanding the debate will help to consider how we assess dyslexia; who we identify as being dyslexic; the kinds of things that we do to remediate dyslexia; and the kinds of adjustments that we can make so that the curriculum, place of study and access to work are easier for people with dyslexia to participate in more fully.

Morgan started the debate by describing a young boy, aged 14, called Percy F (Morgan, 1896). Percy was developmentally very similar to his peers, he was bright and intelligent, good at games and able to solve mathematical problems such as multiplying 749 by 867. His teacher considered him 'the smartest lad in the school if the instruction was entirely oral'. However, Percy had great difficulty with learning to read and spell, despite having private tutors since the age of seven years. So much so, that Morgan wrote in the *British Medical Journal* that he thought that the cause of the problem must be congenital. This way of describing dyslexia echoes around current debates.

- Reading and spelling skills are not developing as well as other skills. There is some recognition now that reading and spelling are different processes and dyslexia could be a weakness in reading alone, spelling alone, or both reading and spelling. There is debate about how different the other skills have to be – some people argue that dyslexia is a difficulty with reading and writing *irrespective of other skills*. Other people argue that a differential diagnosis is needed to distinguish other reasons for poor reading and writing from dyslexia – that is dyslexia is a special case of poor reading or spelling skills. A few people argue that dyslexia as a concept is not very helpful, there is just a difficulty in reading and spelling that can be overcome with good-quality teaching (e.g. Elliott, 2005; Elliott and Gibbs, 2008).

- If it is congenital, then there must be detectable and observable structural differences in the way the brain functions that impact on reading and spelling but not general ability. Many areas of brain function have now been explored and implicated as possible causes. Another implication from this is that even when the reading and writing difficulties have been overcome, there will still be some difficulties that persist in the way that information is processed that will impact on adult life. That is to say, dyslexia is for life. Linked to this notion is the idea that other parts of the brain take over and people with dyslexia develop skills in other areas to compensate for their weaknesses – leading to the term 'compensated dyslexic'.

- Implicit in Morgan's description is that the apparent difficulties are not the result of poor teaching or a lack of opportunity to learn. This has been strengthened in some definitions of dyslexia (e.g. BPS, 1999; Bradley et al., 2005; D. Fuchs et al., 2003). In part this also sets up a debate about the use of medical labels in educational contexts.

- Morgan did not go on to talk about the emotional impact of dyslexia for some learners and the extent to which the educational context and socio-political agendas contribute to some children feeling inadequate as learners. These factors also lead to more children being identified as having difficulties by teachers than might be the case (Squires, 2012; Squires et al., 2012; Squires et al., 2013).

- Morgan did not consider how some of the barriers to learning might be removed and access to learning or work improved through the use of reasonable adjustments; that is, the disabling nature of dyslexia can be increased or reduced through the way in which the social world of learning and work are organised. This is consistent with the social model of disability and the capabilities framework (Burchardt, 2010). The removal of barrier to learning features in an approach used in English schools referred to as dyslexia-friendly (Mackay, 2006). This notion is central to assessments that are carried out to make examinations, study and access to work possible through 'reasonable adjustments', but can be taken further with careful planning that anticipates that learners will be diverse and have different strengths and weaknesses.

Dyslexia or not? Issues from teaching

Reading and writing are given high priorities in education; this has been the case since schools were inspected on their ability to teach the three Rs: Reading, wRiting and aRithmetic (or reading, recording and reckoning).

In more recent years, the driving force for this has been the recognition that good literacy skills underpin economic competiveness (OECD, 2013). This has motivated many governments to attempt to strengthen the curriculum and control the way that literacy is taught and international comparisons are made that rank that country's performance (Mullis *et al.*, 2012). In England this led to the introduction of the National Literacy Strategy (DfEE, 1998) with a tightly defined and prescriptive approach to teaching. Each term in a child's primary school education was mapped out with expected targets to be reached and a mechanism for judging how effectively schools met these targets.

On the positive side, such an approach dealt with a critique that had been levelled at teachers who did not know how to teach literacy. The National Literacy Strategy supported teachers with materials, approaches and ongoing training designed to overcome poor-quality teaching. There was a heavy emphasis on teaching phonics and phonological awareness. On the down side, the National Literacy Strategy expected all children to learn at the same pace, with learning broken down, by teaching tasks, into a daily literacy hour. The success of the National Literacy Strategy can be judged by looking at the attainment levels of children at the end of the primary phase of education. Data published annually by the government shows that the strategy made a slight difference to the percentage of children who were not achieving at expected levels in reading (see Figure 1.1).

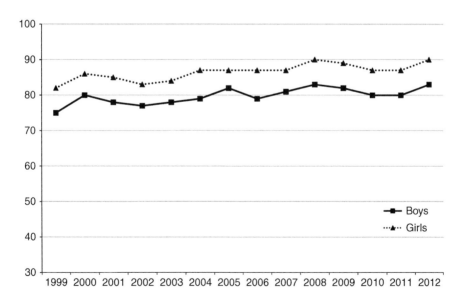

Figure 1.1 Percentage of children reaching expected standards in reading at the end of primary education.

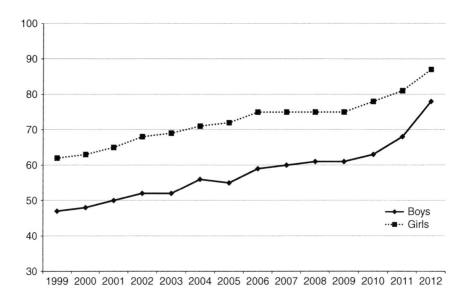

Figure 1.2 Percentage of children reaching expected standards in writing at the end of primary education.

In a 12-year period to 2011, 5 per cent more children were achieving the expected levels in reading. This still meant that 20 per cent of boys and 13 per cent of girls were failing to reach this standard. Significant changes in the way that reading and writing are assessed were introduced in 2012 (DfE, 2013) and this may account for the increase in the final year.

The picture regarding writing looks more favourable, with around 20 per cent more children achieving the expected level (see Figure 1.2). However, in 2011, 19 per cent of girls and 32 per cent of boys failed to reach the standard set out by government.

In both reading and writing, boys appear to be underperforming compared to girls and many reasons for this have been suggested. These include that girls develop language skills earlier than boys, giving them an advantage when it comes to reading; the interest levels of materials used suit girls more than boys; the way that teaching takes place suit the more passive learning style of girls compared to boys. For a while, it was thought that there was a general feminisation of the primary school, with a lack of male role models (Parkin, 2007); however, this view is not supported by other research evidence (Driessen, 2007; Martin and Rezai-Rashti, 2009).

Of course, we would expect reading and writing skills to be normally distributed in the population, with some children doing better than others. There should be an equal spread about the mean, with the majority of

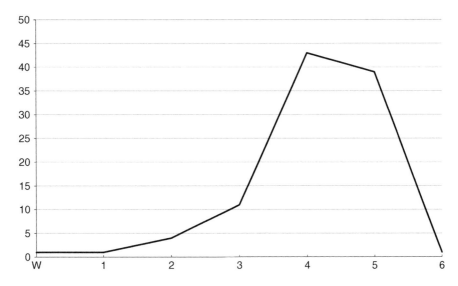

Figure 1.3 Distribution of reading teacher assessments for pupils at the end of the primary school phase in 2012.

pupils in the middle. This is not the case, the distribution is positively skewed. There is a long tail of underachievement (see Figure 1.3).

The concern about the underachieving tail has been around for a while and has led to several targeted approaches to remediate poor literacy-skill acquisition. This is based on the idea that further small group teaching may make up for missed learning opportunities that have arisen for a number of reasons, such as:

- The curriculum pace being too quick for learning to be mastered and generalised, leaving pupils at the acquisition phase with incomplete learning. The small group work allows pace to be matched more closely to pupil learning and provides more opportunities to master concepts and skills. This approach sometimes fails because the learning that is taking place in the small group setting is not generalised through matched learning experiences in the main classroom setting. There needs to be good linkage between the small group work and the rest of the classroom activities.
- Pupil absence and missed learning opportunities. The materials devised for the targeted interventions allow pupils the chance to go over the missed learning.
- Behavioural or attentional difficulties that mean that, although the pupil was in the classroom, they were not accessing the lesson. Smaller groups provide more opportunities for adults to manage the behaviour or pupils' attention, and focus them in on the learning.

There is some emerging evidence that when teachers pay more attention to the needs of children with SEN more generally these children will make more progress as teaching is matched more closely to learning needs. In the Achievement for All national evaluation, children with SEN were able to make more progress than peers in English when teachers were more focused in their approach (Humphrey and Squires, 2011, 2012).

This general shift in how teaching of literacy takes place has resulted in an approach which starts with good teaching for all and then has targeted teaching for small groups of pupils. This still leaves a few pupils for whom more intensive work is needed. The approach is being used in several countries, with slightly different language to describe the same principles. In the UK, teachers talk about 'waves of interventions' in which Wave 1 is referred to as 'quality first' teaching; Wave 2 involves small group programmes and has materials referred to as early literacy support, additional literacy support and further literacy support; Wave 3 involves specific interventions that are tailor-made for individual pupils and written into an individual education plan (IEP), requiring additional adult support. The terminology in Ireland that covers the same levels is friendlier: 'support for all'; 'support for some'; and 'school support plus' (NCSE, 2011a, 2011b; NEPS, 2010). In the US, the same ideas are covered by 'response to intervention' (e.g. see Fox *et al.*, 2009; Jimerson *et al.*, 2007; Klotz and Canter, 2007).

Even with this staged approach and intensive intervention for a few pupils, there seem to be some pupils who are like Pringle Morgan's Percy. They continue to struggle, despite good-quality teaching and a curriculum more closely matched to their learning needs. But it is only after this effort has been made that we can differentiate these children, who may be dyslexic, from those for whom curriculum pace, curriculum structure, missed learning opportunities or behavioural orientation to learning has been the cause of poor reading.

The question about whether these children learn in a qualitatively different way has intrigued educators. Some researchers have pointed to the role of maturation in learning to read. In order to be able to decode the text on the page, the reader needs a stable image with both eyes focused on the same spot. Binocular stability improves with age and this has been regarded as a possible reason as to why children have difficulty learning to read. In studies to explore the effects of 'patching' one eye to occlude vision and strengthen eye muscles, significant improvements were made in reading compared to non-patched children (Stein and Fowler, 1985).

More recent research has suggested that poor eye control may not be the cause of poor reading ability for adult dyslexics (Shovman and Ahissar,

Table 1.1 Development of stable vision (Stein, 1996)

Age (years)	% with binocular stability
6	54
7	70
9	85

2006). This is one possible reason as to why some children outgrow their dyslexia while others do not. It could be that developing better eye control helps some children become better readers, while those who have other underlying causes continue to struggle with developing literacy.

Other researchers have looked at the development of reading sub-skills as children age and found that dyslexic children learn the same sub-skills as non-dyslexic children but at a slower pace (Treiman, 1997). In particular, across different languages the analyses of children's spelling errors shows that they are not random but contain features of the written language to which the children have been exposed – for example, over-using the letters that make up their own name (Pollo *et al.*, 2009). In learning to spell, children move through the same developmental pattern, but dyslexic children take longer.

- Pre-spelling – distinctions are made between scribbling that represents drawings and scribbling that represents letters. The marks may be smaller, or travel in lines similar to the patterns of letters that they have seen in other texts.
- Logographic – particular symbols are associated with particular words. Children learn to recognise their favourite brand names by the pictograms, fonts and ink colour selected by manufacturers.
- Syllabic-grapheme – each syllable is given a single letter. This hypothesis has been around since the 1990s and is at odds with a second hypothesis referred to as the minimum quantity hypothesis, in which children understand that words tend to have more than one letter.
- Grapheme–phoneme correspondence – children learn that letters represent particular sounds found in speech.
- Orthographic spelling – children learn that the sounds each letter represents can be modified by the surrounding letters. There are spelling rules to help deal with common modifications (e.g. the 'magic e' rule transforms short vowel sounds into long vowel sounds).
- Morphemic spelling – the etymology of a word and its meaning are important for preserving spelling patterns, even when the sound of the word changes. Examples include: heal-health; locations such as here–there–where.

This difference in pace of learning suggests that we may simply be categorising some children as having a learning difficulty when all they need is the teaching adjusting to match their learning.

Socio-political influences on identification

There are pressures on teachers to over-identify children as having learning difficulties. One of these pressures arises from the way that schools are judged on the quality of the teaching. Schools in England are judged on how many children reach a politically determined level of attainment. The more children that reach the level, then the better the school is seen to be performing. School performance tables are then published yearly, showing how the school compares to other schools. The underlying assumption is that if children are all equal when they start school, then the level of attainment reached at the end of each phase of education is an indication of the quality of teaching. But children are not equal. They are developmentally different when they start school and there is a normal distribution of all abilities, producing variability in learning rates and in final attainments. At the extreme low end, many of these children are defined as having special educational needs and adjustments have been made to allow the percentage of children with SEN to be taken into account in the school performance tables. This has led to some schools labelling more children with SEN so that the school looks better in terms of the 'league table' position and to a general over-identification of children with SEN to cover up poor-quality teaching (OFSTED, 2010).

A second influence that has been noted is that children who are chronologically younger than their peers within the same age cohort are more likely to be perceived as having special educational needs by their teachers (Squires *et al.*, 2012; Squires *et al.*, 2013) or referred for dyslexia assessments by their parents (Johnson *et al.*, 2013). This is likely to be because the pupils' developmental age is lower when they start school and their language skills, perceptual skills and social skills will be less than that of their peers, so there is a mismatch between teaching and learning. Teachers then see that pupils are not reaching the aspirational targets and consider that the pupils learning is slower than their older peers, leading to these pupils being labelled as having special educational needs. This month of birth effect leads to children born in August being 1.3 times as likely as children born in September to be identified as being dyslexic. When more sophisticated normative assessments are undertaken using psychometric tools, many of these children are then found to be developing normally and found not to have dyslexia. There is no month of birth effect when normative assessments are undertaken.

The third influence comes from the psychometric tools themselves and the misunderstanding of the measures used. Teachers often quote reading ages or spelling ages as indicators of how well a child is doing in literacy. A reading age is set at the point at which half of the children of that particular age can succeed to that point in the test. This means that half perform better and half perform less well. Half of all children aged six years have a reading age of less than six years on any given test. The table below shows the spread of ages that are in the statistically average range for the Wechsler Individual Achievement Test (Harcourt Assessment, 2005).

The spread of achievement on the reading test varies over the age range with the test becoming less sensitive to individual differences as people get older. At the lowest end of the age range the reading age is meaningless because the score is close to the test floor. Getting just one word right is all that is required to get a reading age of four years. Once a child reaches six years of age the test becomes more sensitive and the reading age takes on more meaning. Even here, being four months below chronological age is still within the average range and nothing to be worried about. A child aged 13 years can have a reading age three years below chronological age and still be in the average range. Without understanding this fully, a parent may hear that their child is six months 'behind' in reading and become anxious. Parental anxiety puts pressure on schools to do something more for their child and can also lead to further assessments being undertaken to see if their child is dyslexic. Whether this is something to worry about or not

Table 1.2 Average reading ages by age (years and months)

Age of person being tested (years)	Lower average reading age	Upper average reading age
4	4.00 (test floor)	4.08
5	4.04	5.08
6	5.08	6.08
7	6.04	8.08
8	6.08	10.08
9	7.04	12.00–12.04
10	8.00	13.04
11	8.08	16.00
12	9.08	16.00
13	10.00	16.00
14	11.08	16.00
15	12.04	16.00
16	12.04	16.00
17	12.04	16.00
21	15.00	16.00
30	15.00	16.00
40	15.00	16.00
Over 51	15.00	16.00

depends on the age of the child. For anyone over the age of six years, having a reading age six months less than chronological age is perfectly normal. For adults, the highest reading age that can be measured on this test is a reading age of 16; in this sense we are all 'behind', but there is nothing to worry about. This is important to consider when discussing a student's progress in literacy with other professionals, with that student or with their family.

The fourth influence comes from the way that diagnostic labels are used to access resources or adjustments to educational assessment. Being diagnosed with dyslexia can mean that reading ages are used to make decisions about adjustments in examinations. For instance, most examination boards will only allow a reader in the examination if a 16-year-old child has a reading age less than ten years. Such a reading age for a 16 year old would be below average and the child may well struggle to read a paper, so the provision of an adult to read the text seems justified. A 16-year-old child with a reading age of 11 years would also be below average, but not entitled to a reader in the examination. If the complexity of the text to be read requires a reading age more than ten years then the second child would be at a serious disadvantage in an examination compared to both the majority of peers and to a child who is a poorer reader. This places a moral requirement on examination boards to ensure that the text complexity does not exceed the cut-off point for allowing a reader to support the child undertaking the examination. Under these conditions, the dyslexic reader can demonstrate their knowledge and skills in all subjects across the curriculum.

Reflective questions

If a child is not at the expected level in either reading or writing, does this mean they are dyslexic or could be dyslexic?
Have changing teaching approaches changed the number of pupils who might be considered to be dyslexic?
Are boys more susceptible to dyslexia?
What is the point of assessment over time?
To what extent is dyslexia a social construction and is it a useful construct?
How useful is the notion of reading age?

Neurological causations – a summary of key theories

Some children do struggle to learn to read or spell despite the best efforts of their teachers and parents, even when teaching is broken down into fine gradations and closely matched to learning. This has led to a search for the possible underlying neurological causations using a range of approaches including post mortem studies, brain imagining techniques, developmental studies and psychometric studies (for example, see Heim and Grande, 2012; Squires, 2003). These lead to cognitive models of how information is processed when text is being decoded and understood.

Research adopting perspectives from evolutionary biology and neuropsychology has disclosed that learning to read (as distinct from speaking or listening, i.e. wider 'language' use) is an innovation: an add-on extra borne out of human society and culture rather than an innate, biologically 'hardwired' activity with dedicated networks in the brain.

Dehaene and Cohen (2011) for example, describe how reading is an 'evolutionarily unexpected feat' (p. 260) and explain that 'the human brain cannot have evolved a dedicated mechanism for reading. The invention of writing is too recent and, until the last century, concerned too small a fraction of humanity to have influenced the human genome' (p. 254). From this view it appears that our brains adapt when reading (and when learning to read) using many of the parts of the brain. This includes parts of our brain (cortex) connected with language; the senses; our working memory; and also specialised areas such as the visual word form area (Dehaene and Cohen, 2011). One implication of this important observation is that it suggests that learning to read (and learning to write) for all of us is potentially prone to problems simply because it is not an essential part of our evolutionary, neurobiological makeup. That some individuals experience what is described as dyslexia (or, alternatively, 'literacy difficulties') is, therefore, less surprising when considered in this light.

Several causative theories have now been developed that share the common assumption that there is no single centre in the brain that is responsible for reading. An important limitation of any current theory which seeks to explain dyslexia from a neurobiological explanatory model results from the difficulty of knowing how information flows through the brain and the limits in resolution of imaging techniques. Even if a single neurone could be imaged as information flows through part of the brain, we would not know precisely what that neurone was doing. For instance, the neurone could be decoding letter shape or it could simply be attenuating the neural signal before passing the information onto another area in the brain that decodes letter shape. The extent to which function is localised or function is distributed is not fully understood. However, the different causative theories help us to understand the complexity of the reading process and the number of areas of the brain involved.

The phonological deficit hypothesis

Reading and writing are seen as extensions to spoken communication and are treated as a language skill. The way in which sound is processed is important in translating printed text to spoken sound and to the inner voice. Extensive research has identified a list of phonological processing deficits that have become associated with dyslexia and described as a phonological core deficit (Goswami, 2003).

Sound perception difficulties

- less sensitivity to rhyme and alliteration than reading level-matched controls (Bradley and Bryant, 1978; Bryant and Bradley, 1983);
- difficulty in recognising rhyme and alliteration and analysing words for their constituent sounds – e.g. /k/a/t/ (Hulme and Snowling, 1994, 1997);
- poor phonological decoding rather than poor linguistic comprehension (Snowling et al., 1997).

Phonological loop difficulties in working memory (Baddeley and Hitch, 1974)

A trend between ability in English and working memory has been noted, suggesting that the ability to manipulate sounds and synthesise words is important for six- and seven-year-old children who are learning to read (Alloway, 2011; Gathercole and Alloway, 2008).

- difficulty repeating pseudo-words (Gathercole et al., 1994; Hulme and Snowling, 1994, 1997; Snowling, 1981);
- greater difficulty than peers in repeating polysyllabic words (Hulme and Snowling, 1994, 1997; Miles, 1983);
- repeating random sequences of words or numbers in the correct sequence after hearing them;
- repeating unfamiliar words (Hulme and Snowling, 1994, 1997).

Word fluency

- rapidly naming objects (Hulme and Snowling, 1994, 1997);
- word-finding difficulties and lexical access (Snowling et al., 1997).

Spoken language

- difficulty with speech production and speech perception (Hulme and Snowling, 1994, 1997).

In a small-scale study, eight out of nine poor readers and three out of four poor spellers were found to have weakness in verbal processing (Squires, 2003). Not surprisingly, children who have phonological deficits may also be assessed as having language difficulties such as a specific language impairment (SLI). Approximately half of all children who have an SLI develop dyslexia by the end of Year 2 or Year 3 of primary school (Agnew *et al.*, 2004).

The visual deficit hypothesis

In order to be able to read the words on this page, your eyes have to focus on the letters, light has to enter your eye and then the nervous signal has to be transmitted to the optical cortex and the image processed. Once individual shapes have been made sense of, the meaning attributed to the shapes has to be accessed. Any difficulties in this process are referred to visual deficits. There is a wide variation in how researchers consider the impact that visual deficits have on reading ability. At one extreme, it was found that there was no correlation between children's visual skills and reading ability (Olson, 1989). At the other extreme, visual deficits have been found in up to 75–80 per cent of developmental dyslexics (Lovegrove and Williams, 1993; Slaghuis and Lovegrove, 1985; Talcott *et al.*, 1998).

Earlier we discussed the need for a stable image through good binocular control and that this develops as children age (Stein, 1996). It is also essential that the lens in each eye is clear and there are no cataracts. The lens needs to be able to focus the light onto the retina to produce a clear image. In some people, the lens needs assistance to do this, either through the ageing process or because the eyeball is not perfectly round. These physical requirements ensure that both eyes are looking at the same target and that the image on the retina is as clear as possible.

A second effect that has been noted is linked to the different roles of the light receptors in the centre of the retina and those on the periphery. There is a high concentration of those in the centre of the retina on the fovea and these are responsible for differentiating fine detail and colour perception. Those on the edges of the retina are responsible for movement detection. These two types of receptors play different roles in reading and are processed through different neurological pathways within the visual system (Livingstone and Hubel, 1987; Stein, 1994). Of particular interest to reading are the transient system (concerned with where things are) and the sustained system (concerned with what things are). These are processed through the magnocellular system.

The magnocellular deficit hypothesis

When reading a word, the eye needs to focus on a small amount of text in one go and then shift focus further along the line to focus on the next piece of text. The eyes flick along a line of text in a series of pauses called saccades. With each pause, the eye focuses on five letters ahead of the current position and three letters behind (on average-sized text). The movement of the eye along the line takes about 30ms and the focused pause 250ms. Yet, an experienced reader does not notice this stop-start action; it all seems very smooth. This is dealt with by the magnocellular system, a section of the geniculate body. We are unaware of the saccadic movements because the magnocellular system is able to inhibit vision when the eyes are moving. If it did not do so then we would see a blurred image as the image of the text on the retina rapidly changed. We also have two eyes, each with a slightly different image, both moving. So when the eyes move they must move in a co-ordinated way, move the same distance along the line of text and produce an overlapping image that can be decoded. Some children are unable to do this and this has been linked to a deficit in the magnocellular region. This causes the letters on the page to appear to move or change position, a condition referred to as oscillopsia. For a beginner reader, this is particularly problematic because they need a stable image of a single letter or pair of letters so that they can associate it with a particular phoneme.

   More recent studies have suggested that the magnocellular region may be involved in processing changing stimuli (Holloway *et al.*, 2013; Yamomoto *et al.*, 2013). This means that it will affect perception of changing visual or linguistic stimuli, or both. Impairment of the magnocellular region of the medial geniculate body leads to impaired phonological skills. Impairment of the magnocellular region of the lateral geniculate body leads to impaired ocular control. Impairment in both the medial region and the lateral region will lead to poor visual and auditory perception.

The central executive dysfunction hypothesis

Baddeley and Hitch's model of working memory hypothesised a central executive that is responsible for allocating attention between different cognitive tasks or processes (Baddeley and Hitch, 1974). Since the development of the model, neurological studies have suggested that this might be role undertaken by the frontal lobes. In order to be able to read successfully, the beginner reader needs to be able to focus attention on how the text appears and then shift attention to how the word sounds by blending the different phonemes to make up the word. A weakness in the central executive has been proposed as a possible cause of dyslexia that may explain overlaps with other attentional control conditions such as ADHD (Elliott, 2001).

The cerebellum dysfunction hypothesis

Fluent reading is a well-co-ordinated skill in which eye movement, decoding of text and accessing meaning all seem to occur effortlessly for the mature reader. Watching a child start to learn to read reveals the complexity of this task and how automatic it has become. This is similar to learning many other skills, where there is initially a great deal of cognitive effort until a point is reached when it all becomes automatic. The part of the brain that is involved in automaticity is the cerebellum. A lack of fluency can be attributed to difficulties with making automatic links between different processes and can underpin poor reading (Fawcett and Nicholson, 1999).

Summary of neurological causations

What can be seen from the theories above is not so much that they disagree about causation; rather each is right for *some* dyslexic pupils and adults. Looking through each neurological causation, we can see possible links to other developmental disorders. This explains why some children who are dyslexic may also have been diagnosed with other conditions. It helps us to realise why an intervention that works for one child, may not work for another. It also stresses the importance of careful assessment so that the best teaching interventions can be chosen rather than using a 'one size fits all' approach. Unfortunately, we do not have MRI scanners in schools to explore active brain function so we have to probe cognitive processing using a variety of tasks.

Reflective questions

Is it better to have multiple diagnoses or to carry out a differential diagnosis? Why?
What do the different causal hypotheses suggest about the assessments needed?
How does assessment help in deciding on the type of intervention?
How can the within-child model of neurological explanations for the causation of dyslexia work alongside the social model of disability? In what ways do the two models support each other and in what ways do they create tensions?

Chapter summary

We started this chapter by citing Pringle Morgan's description of young Percy and then investigated the complexity of the social construction of dyslexia. We established that – partly because teachers are under pressure, in many countries, to enable children to reach certain standards, the defining of which inevitably means that some children do not reach them – the issue of whether or not certain children are dyslexic is open to debate. Some will have severe and persistent difficulties, while others will have mild difficulties or difficulties that respond to good-quality teaching interventions.

Child development theories and research tell us that some children will develop slower than other children, and that what can look like substantial and severe difficulties can sometimes resolve themselves through maturation. In some cases, simply being the youngest in the class means that children are less well developed than their peers and that their reading development appears to be behind that of their peers when cohort benchmarks are used. For other children, this is not the case and they may have underlying neurological deficits.

Different neurological perspectives on the cause of dyslexia remind us that affected individuals vary widely in how they experience the phenomena. They can have different strengths and different weaknesses; this has important implications for assessment of dyslexia. Even when reading is improved, some of these strengths and weaknesses will remain, affecting the way that they process all information (not just text). This means that dyslexia is for life and that – even when reading accuracy and spelling accuracy reach acceptable levels – there may still be weaknesses in literacy and working with text. This has implications for the kinds of reasonable adjustments made in examinations and in the workplace.

Chapter 2

Some thoughts on teaching reading

The standard model of reading and dyslexia

Introduction

For many, if not most, individuals affected by dyslexia, difficulty with reading is one of the most disabling features of their educational experience (Burden, 2005; Riddick, 2010; Snowling *et al.*, 2007). This chapter offers considered thoughts on how educators might, therefore, respond to the pressing issue of how to teach reading to learners with dyslexia and facilitate positive progress for affected individuals.

This chapter considers the issue of how educators might work with individuals with dyslexia, starting with a clarification of exactly how they might help typically developing children learn to read. As was highlighted in Chapter 1 ('What is dyslexia?'), acquiring literacy – particularly effective instruction in learning to read – is of major concern to governments and policy-makers internationally (Australian Government, 2005; DfE, 2012 [England]; Ministry of Education, 2007 [NZ]; National Reading Panel, 2000 [US]; Rose, 2006 [England]).

In this sprit we offer an overview of what we describe as a 'standard model of reading', which can be extracted from a range of influential policy documents/initiatives in the UK, US, Australia and New Zealand setting out guidance for how educators should teach early reading to typically developing children. International research that might support these views is also referred to and key concepts used, such as phonological awareness. This is followed by a critical evaluation of how concepts and educational practices suggested by the standard model of reading might (or might not) apply to individuals with dyslexia.

As we will see, setting out how typically developing children acquire reading is itself problematic, feeding through into the decisions and dilemmas which educators face when thinking about how they might support a learner with dyslexia in developing their reading. We suggest that there is no wholly correct or wholly incorrect response to such a multidimensional and contested issue. The view taken by what follows is, rather, that an informed, sceptical consideration of this topic can be helpful for educators in offering a measured response, given the uncertainties which we present.

An open perspective is, therefore, taken and is recommended on this complex issue: one which takes into account the many factors which can influence knowledge, understanding and skills involved in developing or acquiring the ability to successfully read for all individuals. What follows does not offer a 'how to' guide in respect of teaching a child to read: it is presumed that the reader already has access to practical teaching resources of this kind. Rather, we suggest that thinking around some of these wider and deeper issues can best inform the *how* and *why* of classroom practice, including the selection of resources and strategies. We invite our reader to join us in taking an open-minded approach to this topic.

This chapter is designed, therefore, to benefit those who specialise in teaching individuals with dyslexia. However, it should also assist those who teach reading more generally. In every class there will be children who do not have a diagnosed disability, such as dyslexia, but who may nevertheless be 'poor' readers of the kind highlighted in policy documents which refer to underachievement in literacy (Australian Government, 2005; DfE, 2012). The philosophical implication here, in line with this book more broadly, is that the kinds of difficulties for children with dyslexia are not intrinsically different from those faced by their non-dyslexia peers, particularly those typically developing children in the early stages of acquiring reading (although there are significant adjustments that will need to be made to ensure that this is sensitive to the age context of the individual). In Chapter 1 ('What is dyslexia?'), for example, it was suggested that, when learning to spell, children move through the same developmental pattern, but that those with dyslexia take longer and often expend far greater effort than their typically developing peers.

When compared with practice for typically developing children, teaching children with dyslexia to read requires educators to respond, we propose, with greater flexibility in the range and type of strategies or interventions used; greater precision in ongoing evaluation of these strategies; and wider, informed recognition of the many contextual and developmental dimensions implicated in acquiring the ability to read with fluency. We highlight behaviour and motivation, working memory and attention as examples of processes which are of particular importance in developing reading and maintaining progress for children, young people or adults with dyslexia.

Consideration of the practical challenges and pragmatic questions which can arise out of practice is also given in the chapter and alongside an overview of how research might inform it. This is especially valuable because, in our view, many accounts of reading do not adequately highlight the practical, emotional and technical demands placed on teachers engaged in this often challenging endeavour.

The standard model of reading: a summary

Approaches to the teaching of reading follow trends and fashions, with some approaches coming into favour and others being relegated. Over the last 20 years, a 'standard model' to advise educators how to teach reading can be discerned from policy documents; this is influenced by a growing body of international research about reading development (Australian Government, 2005, 2013; DfE, 2012 [England]; Ministry of Education, 2007 [NZ]; National Reading Panel, 2000 [US]; Rose, 2006 [England]).

While there are differences of emphasis, national governments and policy-makers have increasingly promoted variants of this standard model to teachers and enshrined elements of it in different national curricula (the need to standardise reading instruction has even been put forward as one important reason for having a national curriculum). Some critical observers have stressed the politically driven, opportunistic flavour of debates around reading achievement in children, particularly when they are initiated and orchestrated by politicians (Ellis and Moss, 2013). Collectively, policy documents and influential research disclose that the standard model of reading draws on the following related arguments and concepts, which have been simplified here for clarity.

Pre-reading, phonological awareness and reading readiness

A child's phonological awareness involves their ability in 'identifying and manipulating larger parts of spoken language such as whole words, syllables, initial consonants and word chunks at the end of words referred to as onsets and rimes' (Morrow, 2005, p. 44). These have been identified as essential initial ingredients in acquiring reading (Fielding-Barnsley, 2010; Hulme and Snowling, 2013; National Institute of Child Health and Human Development and Early Child Care Research Network, 2005; Rose, 2006; Snowling *et al.*, 2000).

By implication, children who fail to develop an 'explicit' phonological awareness are more likely to develop reading difficulties (National Reading Panel, 2000; Rose, 2009; Shapiro and Solity, 2008; Snowling, 2013; Snowling and Hulme, 2011). Early Years education and pre-school provision has been singled out, by research and legislation internationally, as the setting where the development of phonological awareness can be nurtured. Phonological awareness is an awareness of sounds used in spoken language and is necessary to ensure reading readiness. Practice around phonological awareness in an Early Years setting might involve drawing attention to sounds in predominantly *oral language* through songs, rhyme and other play-based, informal activities which highlight the essential 44 possible sound components (phonemes) in the spoken English language; long and short vowels (including exploring with learners how pronunciation affects vowel use); and consonants. In the UK, this logic has informed national tests (e.g. the Phonics Screening Check), which assess children's early reading readiness. These are designed for five to six year olds at the start of the UK's schooling system (YR1) to assess 'whether individual pupils have grasped fundamental phonics decoding skills, and identify which children may need extra help' (DfE, 2012).

The alphabetic principle and independent readers in English

Phonological awareness is sometimes mistakenly believed by teachers to mean linking sounds to print, partly because this step in learning to read is referred to as phonics teaching. Phonological awareness aids beginner readers when they first become aware of written (orthographic) language and in cementing their understanding that the shapes (graphemes) written down (a, b, c, sh, th, cat, dog, mum, dad) represent particular sounds (phonemes) with associated meanings. This emerging knowledge is described as the 'alphabetic principle': the ability to 'crack the code' and map sounds and sound combinations onto written combinations from the English alphabet with increasing skill and fluency (Snowling and Hulme, 2011). Different terms are found in the literature to describe this process of linking graphemes to phonemes; it has been called 'grapho-phonics' or forming 'grapheme–phoneme correspondence'.

Children have to learn that a specific letter shape is associated with a specific sound. They have to link a visual pattern to a sound pattern. This requires good visual and auditory processing, as well as an ability to smoothly shift attentional capacity between the two types of processing. In addition, children start to learn how letters are combined to represent combinations of sounds that are found in words. Blending techniques require each sound to be held in the child's phonological loop, while visual attention is moved to the next letter and this is decoded as a single sound and added to the sound already in the phonological loop ('c-a-t' becomes the smoothly decoded and blended 'cat' for a child reading). This places heavy demands upon developing working memory. Short-term memory capacity limits the amount of sounds that can be held at any one time and, therefore, the length of word that can be blended.

As children develop their decoding and blending skills they are able to approach new words that they have not seen before. Teaching involves further development of skills – for example, using sentence context and meaning to notice errors in decoding and allowing self-correction. In this way the child is able to become their own teacher – the more reading they do, the more successful they become (Fielding-Barnsley, 2010; Share, 1995). Early readers become increasingly *independent* in reading.

Some dyslexic children are very good at using phonological knowledge to help them spell words. They suffer from a phonological regularity effect and try to spell all words as they sound. One of the problems with this approach is that written language does not map consistently onto spoken language. In English there are 44 phonemes but only 26 graphemes. This means that the same sound can be represented by different letter combinations and the same letter combinations can represent different sounds. In some languages some letters are silent and do not map onto any sounds (e.g. gh in ghandek in Maltese; k and w in know). This affects different languages to different extents and is referred to as the 'transparency' of the language. Written UK English is about 85 per cent transparent. In some countries, attempts have been made to simplify spellings to increase the transparency of the language (e.g. in US English, 'colour' has become 'color'). Children have to be taught all of the variations of grapheme–phoneme correspondences in order to deal with irregularly spelled words. Take an example of the word 'ghoti', which has been written here in a way that is phonetically correct but uses the most unusually occurring grapheme–phoneme correspondences from English spelling. Let us break it down for you:

- gh sounds out /f/ as in enou**gh**;
- sounds out /i/ as in w**o**men;
- ti sounds out /sh/ as in sta**ti**on.

Another problem with phonological approaches is that the same meaning unit or morpheme often retains its spelling but changes its pronunciation; for example,

- heal and **health**;
- know and **know**ledge;
- locations such as here, **there**, **where**.

With increasing experience comes increasing fluency with reading. Words that once needed to be segmented and sounds blended can now be recognised as whole words, without the need to decode each grapheme–phoneme correspondence. This early vocabulary starts with simple, one- or two-syllable concrete words referring to the child's immediate environment, such as 'mum', 'dad' and 'school'. For typically developing children, this sight vocabulary quickly grows in size and in the complexity of words automatically recognised (Shapiro *et al.*, 2013). A key part of a teacher's role at this stage is to encourage and support the child's knowledge of common or high-frequency words, recording the child's ability to read and recognise an expanding circle of words. The benefit to the reader is that reading is quicker, more fluent and more efficient. A more automatic decoding process also frees up attentional capacity and memory resources to help the reader to understand what has been read.

For the typically developing child, there is a move from the tiring and efficient letter by letter decoding used at the earliest stages of reading (Farrington-Flint *et al.*, 2008; Watts and Gardner, 2013) to a more automatic and fluent style of reading.

Phonics and synthetic phonics: a key method for teaching reading

We have already said that phonics is different from phonological awareness. Phonics is the educational practice of supporting a child's alphabetic principle (the mapping process) by highlighting letter–sound correspondences. There are different approaches to phonics teaching (Johnston *et al.*, 2012). The favoured instructional form for teaching reading is synthetic phonics (DfE, 2012; National Institute of Child Health and Human

Reflective questions

What are the implications for assessing:

- hearing and sight?
- phonological awareness?
- working memory?
- attentional control?
- short-term memory capacity?
- visual reasoning skills?

How might you encourage parents of very young children to develop phonological awareness in their children? What kinds of games and activities would you recommend? How might this help when the child starts school?

Development and Early Child Care Research Network, 2005; National Reading Panel, 2000; Rose, 2006, 2009).

This teaches children to convert letters (graphemes) into sounds (phonemes) and forms recognisable words from this conversion (National Reading Panel, 2000; Rose, 2006; Wyse and Styles, 2007). At least in the early stages, certain words might be given in isolation and without reference necessarily to texts of any kind (Rose, 2006). Instruction should also be explicit, rigorous and systematic (Mesmer and Griffith, 2005). Any texts which are given at this stage should be entirely decoded by phonemic methods (these contain no words which are irregular – which cannot be 'sounded out' easily: c-a-t, d-o-g, t-a-p) and might be given to children to encourage them to learn the synthetic phonic method of reading (DfE, 2011).

Sounding out and blending should be used in instruction based on synthetic phonics and where children, typically:

> Learn a few letter sounds e.g. 's', 'a', 't', 'p' … and then see whole words made up from these letters e.g. *tap*, *pat* and *sat*. They [children] are not told what these words are, however, but have to sound and blend the letter–sound sequences to read the words independently.
> (Johnston *et al.*, 2012, p. 1371, emphasis original)

An alternative approach uses onset and rime. Rather than splitting each word into component letter sounds, the word is split into two components. This allows children to learn a block of text and reduces demands on working memory. For example, c/at, p/at and s/at all have a common rime.

Teachers' knowledge and understanding of how children learn to read

Teachers themselves should understand how to instruct children who are early readers in explicit, rigorous and systematic synthetic phonics, calling upon an educator's clear personal knowledge of key concepts, such as the alphabetic principle and phonemes in the written English language (DfE, 2011; Fielding-Barnsley, 2010; Mahar and Richdale, 2008). In understanding reading comprehension as a component of reading, educators might also call upon the 'simple view of reading' (Carroll *et al.*, 2011; Hoover and Gough, 1990; Rose, 2009), which stresses that decoding is vital to a child's understanding of what he or she reads, but that, once this is done, he or she falls back upon 'his or her *oral* language comprehension to understand what a writer conveys' (Carroll *et al.*, 2011, p. 10, our emphasis). Some research on reading, which calls on the 'simple view of reading', has suggested that the teaching of reading needs to be supported by developing spoken comprehension skills (Kendeou *et al.*, 2009).

Tiered intervention, RTI and waves for children who do not respond to explicit, rigorous and systematic synthetic phonics

Some children struggle to learn to read despite explicit, rigorous and systematic whole-class instruction in synthetic phonics and are at risk of 'literacy failure' (Hatcher *et al.*, 2006). These children need to spend more time being taught the basic skills and this is arranged in a tiered response system (or 'waves'), which increases the intensity of evidence-based intervention(s) according to the student's response (Rose, 2009). Interventions are tiered from adaptations to whole-class teaching (differentiation) to small group work through to individualised intensive teaching. There is a tension between using approaches to enable children who learn slowly to 'catch up' with more advanced peers and using approaches that consolidate learning and ensure mastery before trying to teach new concepts and skills. Research has focused on these different aspects of teaching and learning, studying how i) a child's performance and skill in recognising and manipulating phonemes (sounds) in common, regular words after small group tutoring outside of the whole class (Gilbert *et al.*, 2013) and ii) how a cohort of children deemed to be behind their peers in reading level respond in their ability to read 30 high-frequency ('common') words as part of an early literacy programme designed to help them catch up a level of their reading (Hatcher *et al.*, 2006). Studies of early intervention show mixed but encouraging results on the effectiveness of a tiered approach to children who do not respond to what has been, for the majority of their peers, high-quality, effective instruction in reading (Snowling and Hulme, 2011; Vaughn and Fletcher, 2012).

The general principle of adapting the teaching to the needs of the child and then seeing how the child responds has been called 'response to intervention' (RTI) in the US (Fox *et al.*, 2009; Fuchs and Vaughn, 2012; Gersten and Dimino, 2006; Klotz and Canter, 2007; Vaughn and Fletcher, 2012). It means that assessment can be linked to the types of teaching undertaken and that teaching can be modified further as a result of the assessment, resulting in a curricular focus around what is taught, how it is taught, what is learned and how quickly. This is very different to previous approaches that saw the assessment as needing to measure how different the child was from peers using standardised instruments that were removed from actual teaching. In the US, RTI is now an established mode of intervention with links to federal legislation around the education of children with what is termed 'reading disability' in the US or who are at risk of failing to acquire literacy (Hallahan *et al.*, 2012). This model also appears in Australia, in emerging education policy focused on meeting the needs of children with dyslexia (Australian Government, 2013, Recommendation 6).

Evidence-based evaluation of educational intervention and practice around teaching children to read

There is a call to evaluate reading programmes and reading interventions of all types in a robust and scientific way (Australian Government, 2013; National Reading Panel, 2000; Rose, 2006). In principle, this would lead us to understanding the approaches that work well for most children when taught under optimum conditions. There are similar calls to evaluate interventions for children who struggle to read (Australian Government, 2013; Goldacre, 2013; Snowling and Hulme, 2011). Such research provides one level of evidence to inform classroom practice. However, we have already explained that the reading process is complex and that children are varied. This means that research has to be carefully constructed to ensure that like is compared with like and that findings are not overly generalised. For instance, generally speaking, a lot of research suggests that those children who have phonological difficulties will have difficulties in reading and that interventions to improve phonological awareness will help. However, not all children who have difficulties in reading have phonological difficulties and, for them, any interventions will be ineffective. A study in the Netherlands with 100 pre-school (kindergarten) children at risk of dyslexia examined whether phonological awareness was a predictor of subsequent difficulty with reading. It found that there was no support for the theory that a deficit in phonological awareness caused the reading deficit in those children who went onto have reading difficulties. Of those with reading difficulties, 80 per cent did not have a phonological deficit in kindergarten (Blomert and Willems, 2010). Educators have a role to play in identifying which intervention is most likely to work with a particular child in a given context. There is a need to translate research findings into classroom practice.

Stages in reading development for typical children

What you might see as an educator

When thinking about the practicalities of helping children to read, some awareness of the broad stages of early reading development is useful. The following sections suggest the way in which these broad periods might appear in typically developing children whose first language is English. They set out what you would usually see in children at each of these approximate stages, referring to terms and concepts in the 'standard model'. These are not exhaustive, but might be helpful in thinking about typically developing children, in contrast to the atypically developing student with dyslexia.

Pre-reading word and phoneme awareness (approximately three to five years)

At this stage, children are becoming increasing aware of sounds (phonemes) in spoken units of language – a quality described as 'phonemic awareness' – and begin to be able to explicitly identify and later manipulate words and word parts in spoken language. Learning around words and sounds should be 'fun' and firmly located within the domain of play. The educator can facilitate increasing confidence, knowledge and awareness among children in 'language' through attention to word sounds (sssssnake ssss) and word/letter shapes as part of fun play activities. Rhyme, rhythm and basic forms in written language can be highlighted by the educator as part of activities. Letters can, for example, be modelled in clay and painted on paper using different colours as part of artwork (or rainbow writing) and as a connection between reading and writing. Often, at this stage, children's motor skills are still developing and the fine motor skills (e.g. precise control of the pencil, pen, crayon) used in handwriting can be a challenge.

By the end of this period children should be prepared for more formal and systematic instruction in learning to read. They might also have a small but growing 'sight vocabulary': a basic list of words they recognise (including, for example, recognising the written form of their first name and words describing their favourite types of animal). Helping children to be able to concentrate, work together on their literacy and listen carefully are vital preparation skills to help with their reading (and other wider aspects of study). The importance of these wider study skills (including a child's limited ability to concentrate at this point) should not be underestimated; they are particularly significant when designing activities to support early reading. A vital task for the educator is to offer children an explicit, predictable but fun framework for developing these study skills involving attention and cognition (Mesmer and Griffith, 2005). Parents and caregivers can support this process by, for example, regularly reading age-appropriate stories to children. These might be chosen by children themselves with parental guidance and become part of a 'bedtime' ritual.

Early reading (approximately five to seven years)

This period offers children a springboard for rapid growth in their abilities. During this time children come to recognise and increasingly be able to predict the correspondence (or connections) between letters/groups of letter and corresponding sounds. This important new ability is described as the 'alphabetic principle' or 'alphabetic code' (or as graphophonic mapping).

Initially, this process is carried out through labour-intensive (and very tiring) decoding, where the child will sound out every letter: c-a-t; d-o-g; m-u-m; d-a-d. A large strain is put on the child's working memory (see Topic 8) at this point as they decode each sound (phoneme) and its corresponding shape (grapheme) on the page.

Reading at this early stage is often still inaccurate and children will frequently hesitate when they experience new, unusual or *phonetically irregular words* (words which cannot be easily sounded out). At this stage, a child has a still limited but growing sight-reading vocabulary: these are words which they can recognise on sight and read without having to decode each letter. To begin with, words in this group are one or two syllables long – they become increasingly long and complex as the child's confidence and abilities grow. For educators who are teaching reading this important stage in a child's reading development can often require the most input and most effort; children can also experience tiredness and even frustration as they grapple with these new skills and knowledge. Educators can encourage children at this point by, for example:

- drawing in the support and encouragement of that child's family and/or carers: in some cases the family members may need support for their literacy – for example, if in they hail from a disadvantaged social group or if English is a second/additional language (EAL/D);
- ensuring that reading is a regular, predictable but fun part of each day;
- offering books and other reading materials which are structured to help children's early reading – in the early stages these will have simple (one- or two-syllable) words in short, simple sentences, supported by appropriate images to aid the child's prediction;
- helping the child to make meaning from their reading by working through comprehension questions related to the text, such as 'What happened when ...?';

- ensuring that children feel able to make good progress and 'do well'/are motivated no matter what level their reading is at;
- identifying, in concert with colleagues, which children might require additional support with learning to read. This support can vary between temporary additional help with a specific aspect of reading (decoding, comprehension) and extensive intervention, involving other specialists, when a child is making no appreciable progress in learning to read.

There has been some suggestion that teaching synthetic phonics might be beneficial for reading development at this stage and in order to offer explicit instruction for children to help them better predict letter–sound correspondence. Synthetic phonics are where the child is intensively introduced to (only) phonetically regular words, which are not in the context of a sentence and where the emphasis is on decoding the sound–letter correspondence. This approach has caused much debate and disagreement involving educators, parents, scholars/researchers and policy-makers.

By the end of this period children emerge with a self-correcting mechanism: they can self-correct errors made in reading (often these are accompanied by a pause or the child will reread the word correctly).

Consolidation of reading (approximately seven years and above)

From this point on, typically-developing children consolidate and extend the knowledge and skills they have already gained. They will increasingly be confident to read words and simple sentences from their wider environment (at home and in the community); they can read a menu written in English in a restaurant; and read many adverts on billboards. This can often provoke questions about the content and meaning of sentences or meaning of unfamiliar words. When a child reads aloud, the tone of what they read often improves at this point and has less hesitation compared to how it was previously: reading has become automatic and far less cognitive processing effort is required to read (Armstrong and Squires, 2014).

Children rely far less on sounding out words and can smoothly blend what they read: 'c-a-t', for example, becomes 'cat'. Children can successfully read and understand sentences of an increasingly complex type (compound complex sentences). Errors made are often auto-corrected by the child as they figure out how to use what they already know to predict how to read unfamiliar words or phrases. The child is established as a reader; it is simply the complexity and sophistication of what they read which now increases in late childhood, through into late adolescence and beyond.

Observations on the standard model of reading

The standard model of reading as outlined here is a simplified amalgam drawn from policy literature and pronouncements in the UK, US, Australia and New Zealand referring to how teachers might (or in some cases, e.g. DFE [2011], 'should') teach reading to young children. However, the way that the model is implemented and the extent to which teachers apply explicit, systematic phonics instruction varies on many levels. There are differences in local practices, within schools and even between individual teachers (Mesmer and Griffith, 2005).

Reflective questions

Do any of the practices you use in teaching reading (such as an emphasis on letter sounds in words) call on/derive from elements of the simple view of reading model?

Does it appear familiar in offering a (persuasive?) narrative or story about how children learn to read and what an educator's role(s) might be here?

In your context, are waves or intervention or RTI influential upon practice? Is the intensity of interventions around reading, writing or literacy based, in any sense, on a student's response to instruction?

How are interventions modified as a result of assessing the child's development in reading and spelling?

The standard model of reading appears to be appealing for policy-makers and some teachers. However, aspects of it, notably the promotion of synthetic phonics for teaching early reading, have attracted considerable criticism from researchers, scholars and educators. In a detailed examination of studies used to support the use of synthetic phonics in teaching reading, Wyse and Styles (2007), for example, argue that the Rose reports view that synthetic phonics should be adopted as the preferred method for the teaching of early reading is not supported by the research evidence. Other educationalists have commented that synthetic phonics is a 'monstrous regime' and argued that it is a politically motivated 'universal imposition of teaching strategies' rather than one based on evidence (Davis, 2012, p. 562).

Alongside disagreement on the implications of research for teaching reading there is also indication that the findings and implications of research into reading have, themselves, been compromised or lost in their travel from research paper to policy-maker or educator. The phrase 'lost in translation' seems pertinent when thinking about some research in this area and its presentation in policy around teaching reading and other areas of education (Armstrong, 2013). For example, the 'simple view' of reading had first been outlined by Gough and colleagues in 1986 and in 1990 (Gough and Tunmer, 1986; Hoover and Gough, 1990). It was referred to by Stainthorp and Stuart in 2006, for Rose's *Independent Review of the Teaching of Early Reading*, almost 20 years later. Their reflective public article, because of its inclusion in the influential Rose publication, suddenly itself became well known – spawning over 260 research articles discussing it between 2006 and 2008 – and attracted the eye of policy-makers at an international level (Stainthorp and Stuart, 2008). They suggest that while the model might have more grounding in research than other models of reading it is primarily a helpful, 'clear conceptual framework within which teachers can organise their thoughts' (Stuart *et al.*, 2008). Uncritical adoption of the model by policy-makers when they consider reading and promotion of it to educators as 'evidence-based' ignores the fact that the model is simply intended as a stimulus for thought and discussion.

Reflective questions

The prevalence and promotion of the standard model of reading creates an important potential quandary for our reader.
   This dilemma occurs on two related levels:

- How, if at all, is the standard model of reading relevant to learners who present with or who are at risk of dyslexia?
- What might constitute a reasoned, 'evidence-informed' response by educators in this situation and in supporting reading for individuals who appear to have dyslexia?

In the rest of this chapter, we consider possible answers to these two reflective questions and invite our reader to reflect further on what we propose in light of their own experience.

The problem

Despite the research and the models of reading presented, we do not really know how children learn to read. There are currently few research studies which involve individuals with dyslexia, which also examine what might constitute effective educational practice in helping them to read (Snowling and Hulme, 2011). This is at least partly because the theoretical frameworks around how we develop reading are, more generally, unclear or are contested. For most children, the process seems to occur naturally, almost despite the approaches used by teachers. Some authors have gone so far as to say that there is no single overarching theory of how reading is acquired (Elliott and Gibbs, 2008). That there is, as yet, no agreed, clear idea of how typically developing children acquire the ability to read is contrary to confident pronouncements often in the media emanating from governments or private corporations/educational publishers in the US, UK, Australia and elsewhere. These statements often (over)confidently imply that their particular approach or programme is based on a clear understanding of how children learn to read and a robust 'evidence-base'. In their perceptive account of questionable terms often associated with the term 'evidence-based', Mesmer and Griffith (2005, p. 366, emphasis original) comment: 'As reading teachers we are often frustrated by the fads and extremes that tend to plague our field ... In materials for beginning reading instruction, the essential label is *explicit, systematic, phonics instruction.*' They critically add, 'For the past several years this phrase has been attached to almost every beginning reading product.' In these circumstances, whether the standard model of reading can be truly described as 'evidence-based' is, at best, unclear. It is important to stress that much of the research the standard reading model calls upon for legitimacy refers to typically developing children in the early years. We know even less about atypical children such as those with dyslexia.

Until such times as there is robust 'evidence' in this sphere, it is wise, we think, to refer to 'research-informed' rather than 'evidence-based' practice around reading: anything more certain would be simply unwise and probably unscientific, given the uncertain state of scholarly knowledge in this area. When thinking about what concepts might inform a specialist teacher's practice in teaching reading there are wider advantages to adopting a research-informed and as opposed to an evidence-based view of the role of research. A similar situation occurs in the context of adolescent counselling, which is useful in thinking about this problem and in selecting a research-informed view:

> This is not to challenge the potential that evidence-based models have, but to acknowledge that there are other avenues which may prove more fruitful and first, reflect real-world scenarios more accurately, and second, provide a more rounded response to young people who are seeking support.
>
> (Hanley *et al.*, 2012, pp. 1–2)

In educational practice, approaches associated with the influential standard model of reading might risk a negative effect in practice on those that have dyslexia, if applied on a 'one size fits all' basis. A mechanistic way of teaching reading based on task analysis risks forgetting that the true purpose of reading is for pleasure or to gain information. This risk may make reading boring or tedious and create negative, demotivating associations among learners, particularly among boys (Marshall, 2012). This insight is highly relevant, given the negative associations and demotivation reported by a range of research which has examined how older learners or adults with dyslexia feel about reading on account of their difficulties learning to read in education (Armstrong and Humphrey, 2009; Burden, 2005; Riddick, 2010). In many cases individuals reported how reading was not pleasurable precisely because it was a dreaded chore at school, leading them to avoid reading and facing a consequent decline in skill level (Riddick, 2010).

Synthetic phonics may not be the best approach to use with some children with dyslexia. It requires memorisation of letter strings, outside of the contextual cues and clues which might scaffold memorisation (Davis, 2012; Johnston *et al.*, 2012; Rose, 2006). There is robust, consistent evidence from experimental studies that many individuals with dyslexia and many other types of associated disability have weaknesses in working memory (Beneventi *et al.*, 2010; Vellutino *et al.*, 2004; Wang and Gathercole, 2013). Indeed, this correlation is so strong that testing working memory has become a standard feature of assessment for dyslexia (see Chapter 3, 'Identification and assessment'). If a weakness in working memory is identified in a diagnostic assessment then instruction can be shaped to avoid overloading and aid memorisation of letter–sound combinations and vocabulary (Alloway, 2011; Gathercole and Alloway, 2008). An emphasis on supporting memory is likely to be most useful in the context of developing reading where, for example, learners are developing an effective sight vocabulary (common or high-frequency words recognised on sight) and in order to move beyond the laborious, demotivating decoding of individual letters.

The standard model of reading is, in many respects, a skills-based account (e.g. decoding skills; phonological skills; instructional skills). Perspectives on teaching and learning that take this view understate or, more often, ignore the complex, ongoing developmental processes which underpin their successful acquisition. Consequently, when learners fail to develop these skills or develop them atypically, there is no wider conceptual frame to suggest why this might have happened or offer an informed perspective on what we might actually do about it: for educators, this situation can be immensely frustrating and unhelpful.

For instance, when we note an individual's difficulty with 'decoding skills' (recognising and decoding letters accurately), the standard reading model takes us no further than implying that the reader is at an early stage of reading development and that if these skills do not improve the individual is likely to face major obstacles to becoming a fluent reader. This account does not, of itself, indicate whether what we observe is due to weaknesses in visual processing (Vellutino *et al.*, 2004); processing sounds such as a phonological deficit (Snowling, 1981; Snowling *et al.*, 2000; Snowling and Hulme, 2011; Snowling *et al.*, 1997); working memory (Wang and Gathercole, 2013); or is associated, in fact, with a specific language impairment which also affects their language in other ways such as oral, aural, expressive, or receptive language (Fraser *et al.*, 2010). These are vital questions, however, in considering whether and to what extent a child might have dyslexia, how this might, precisely, affect their reading (as part of identification and effective assessment) and also what we should practically do to assist this individual. In the case of observing poor decoding skills in an individual, should the educator, for example:

- recommend to the individual that they have an eye-test by an optometrist?
- advocate and carry out supplemental and intensive phonological training (Shapiro and Solity, 2008)?
- follow 'a robust framework of memory support which minimises the adverse impact of working memory failure' (Gathercole and Alloway, 2008, p. 92)?
- enquire whether the individual has been assessed by a speech and language therapist and, if so, exactly what kind of therapy has taken place?

These are the kind of concrete questions which inform what a professional does next, but they are not accommodated by the standard model of reading.

A meaningful response to the problem?

So what are we left with? Here are suggestions about what a research-informed approach might consist of and how it might shed light on the teaching of reading to those with dyslexia.

A realistic starting point should be the acknowledgement that there is no 'one size fits all' approach to teaching reading which will benefit all or even most individuals with dyslexia. This implies that a range of strategies, approaches and interventions might be fruitful and that some will be more, or less, applicable at different points in a student's development or in different educational contexts. A highly scholarly review of neuroscience and reading supports this view, highlighting that a response to the simplistic question of 'What works?' depends on many factors that we have already discussed. The authors add:

> As experienced teachers know, no method will work for everyone in a given class, and nothing works for anyone all the time. Given that, the question should probably be rephrased as, What works for particular kinds of students, under particular circumstances, to particular ends, with particular dependability?
>
> (Hruby and Goswami, 2011)

Flexibility and adaptability are also, therefore, highly helpful attributes to have in supporting students with dyslexia as they develop their reading (writing and study). As part of this open-minded strategy, it might be that elements of the standard model are useful in practice and in the planning and application of educational interventions with learners who face challenges in their reading. For example, it is conceivable that, for many reasons, early key aspects of literacy acquisition, such as the alphabetic principle, were disrupted or prevented from developing for a child at that time. In these circumstances, it *might* be beneficial for educators to revisit these in practice and in an age-appropriate manner which is mindful of the fact that these early processes need to be sensitively scaffolded so as to avoid them being seen by the learner as insulting or implying that the learner is immature.

A research-informed approach acknowledges that the instructional strengths, skills and knowledge of the practitioner are essential factors for the progress of learners (Hanley *et al.*, 2012). Language used in policy and research literature to describe children who have significant difficulties with reading often focuses on their deficiencies – for example, literacy failure (Hatcher *et al.*, 2006); poor literacy (DFE, 2012); or phonological deficit (Snowling and Hulme, 2011). One unfortunate by-product of this focus on the affected child (or young person or adult) is that the important role and influence of the educator can be underplayed. Some researchers have even suggested that, in certain contexts, this deficit approach has been used with children who have disabilities (particularly, but not exclusively ADHD) to conveniently divert blame away from the inflexible nature of educational systems in the UK, the US and elsewhere (Cooper, 2008).

Intrapersonal and interpersonal factors

It increasingly appears from research that wider cognitive, psychological and social processes around learning are highly important in the acquisition of reading and of literacy more generally, but far less understood than the development of specific literacy skills (Hirvonen *et al.*, 2010). Contrary to the focus on skill acquisition implied by the standard model of reading, teaching reading to individuals with dyslexia is not simply about acquiring, mastering and generalising technical skills. Progress, instead, often boils down to the adopted coping strategies, pragmatism and sheer tenacity of teacher and learner.

The educator's level of energy, their level of emotional commitment to the goals set and resilience to difficulty or even failure are often vital factors in helping children with dyslexia develop their reading and writing. There is growing research to support this emphasis on the attributes of the teacher when thinking about the progress of children with a disability. This includes:

- the educator's sense of personal efficacy and their estimation of personal influence/power to positively affect the situation (Gibbs, 2007; Poulou and Norwich, 2002; Tschannen-Moran and Woolfolk Hoy, 2007);
- children's estimation of their teachers' personal warmth with increased scholarly achievement (Cooper, 2011).

The demands placed on the teacher, as well as the student, should not be underestimated when helping pupils with dyslexia develop reading skills.

It is also worth recognising, in a holistic way, that there are a host of practical factors which can, often significantly, influence progress in reading and which are not strictly about acquiring or developing the technical, skills-based aspects of reading. These factors include, for example, the student's capacity for additional work on their reading during the day and also homework involving reading. The sheer amount of additional mental energy expended in doing tasks that are not fluent and automatic takes its toll. 'By the end of the day a dyslexic child is generally more tired than his peers because everything requires more thought, takes longer and does not come easily ... The amount and type of homework should therefore be carefully considered' (Pollock and Walker, 1994, p. 148).

Learners might not engage with the interventions aimed at their reading (Armstrong and Humphrey, 2009), or their teacher might struggle to maintain the energy necessary to carry these through, day after day, week after week. Patchy or poor attendance can also be a major issue for educators working with children who have or who are at risk of dyslexia, particularly where such children are also categorised as having forms of SEBD or other disabilities affecting their scholarly performance, behaviour and understanding (Burden, 2005). Why children fail to attend school is, of course, a complex phenomenon which varies widely in its prevalence, from setting to setting and from student to student (Hallam and Rogers, 2008). However, poor attendance can have a highly disruptive effect on efforts directed to help that individual acquire or develop their reading. This disruption can manifest itself at various levels. The child, adolescent or adult involved is often demotivated upon their return, particularly when they learn that their reading skills have either not progressed or have slightly declined; educators themselves become frustrated and often increasingly pessimistic about the prospects of progress for a repeatedly absent learner. Teachers often become particularly demotivated when they have spent hours preparing instructional materials for a high-quality, high-intensity session tailored to a student's specific needs at that point in a sequential reading programme and that student is absent.

The way in which an individual feels about themselves as a learner also affects the amount of effort that they will invest in learning. This can lead to a vicious cycle as negative feedback about performance causes the learner to feel less able and to take fewer risks in learning. This, in turn, reduces performance and leads to further negative comments or negative self-comparisons with peers. For example, 'John's story' in the Introduction to this book captures how this can, in our experience, affect individuals on several levels.

An international review of programmes for children with severe and persistent literacy difficulties highlighted the key role played by these wider factors in reducing the effectiveness of interventions (Griffiths and Stuart, 2013). Interventions can be outstanding, but will still be ineffective if the learner is absent, unmotivated, disengaged or simply unable to consistently concentrate and attend to what they need to learn.

Team around the educator: recognising the demands of teaching reading to learners with dyslexia

In considering these often problematic wider factors around the practice of teaching reading, one practical implication disclosed is the need to support specialist teachers in their efforts with individuals who present with dyslexia. It is vital that the challenges of teaching reading in this context are recognised by the educator's immediate and also more senior colleagues/managers/setting leaders. One-to-one, high-intensity reading instruction, of the kind envisaged by Wave 3 interventions in the UK and as part of RTI in the US, is particularly demanding for delivering educators as well as for learners involved. In this sense, it might be helpful to promote a 'team around the teacher' approach - not in any sense replacing the team around the child approach – but, instead, in realistic recognition of the level of professional and institutional support which practice of this kind entails.

On a final point, whereas a 'one size fits all' approach to reading instruction is probably not helpful for many individuals with dyslexia, the opposite is true for highly specific interventions tailored to meet their exact needs. As highlighted in Chapter 1 ('What is dyslexia?'), there is emerging research from the wider field of disability and special education which discloses that greater progress is often achieved for learners when educators are more focused in their approach (Humphrey and Squires, 2011, 2012).

This leads to the question of how to identify focused strategies and interventions around reading for those who present with dyslexia which, in turn, suggests the need for a careful, high-quality, considered diagnostic assessment. Indeed, this is arguably the essential element of research for practitioners to consider when designing and implementing any interventions intended to support reading for learners with dyslexia. It is also the subject of the next chapter.

Chapter 3

Identification and assessment

In this chapter, we are going to start by considering two questions that we will then expand upon. The two questions remind us about useful points for educators to keep in mind regarding the values, principles and practice of identification and assessment for dyslexia. In keeping with the rest of this book, we critically frame this topic for the reader, encouraging you to consider some of the possible factors which might constrain or enable this key area of practice in *your* local or national context.

Q1 Why assess?

In considering assessment, we first need to ask ourselves why we are assessing. This might sound relatively straightforward: to help individuals with dyslexia learn more effectively. Educators need to know exactly *how* each individual is affected by dyslexia. What could be simpler? At several levels, the reality of this process is often more complicated. To some extent this is so because of wider (social, cultural and philosophical) issues around the purposes of assessment and its impact on the nature of the assessment undertaken.

Sometimes assessment is undertaken simply to give a label. The label acts like an explanation for why a child is not learning to read or spell as well as peers. It calms parents and teachers but offers nothing more. Why does using a term like 'dyslexia' seem to have this affect whereas using the term 'slow reader' or 'poor speller' does not? Partly, this is a convention that we have grown used to in our society where an assessment carried out by a specialist that leads to a medical-sounding name is more valued than a straightforward description. It is like going to the doctor with back pain and coming out of the surgery with lumbago. Nothing has changed, it hurts as much but there is now a name for the condition. There are specialists around who will fulfil this need – but is assessment that is carried out solely for this purpose a good assessment?

Other reasons for assessment are more pertinent. These include:

- Assessing pupil progress when interventions are carried out. This is important because dyslexia can be used as a descriptive label and a child may be given the label at one point in time; after successful teaching, the label may no longer apply.
- The bureaucratic systems used for allocation of resources within schools, so that some pupils receive support or materials and others do not, may require an assessment to help decision-makers. There are some interesting ethical questions around this: if two children have the same reading levels, but one is diagnosed as being dyslexic and the other not, should only one of them receive support? Assessments in the UK differentiate between specific learning difficulties and general learning difficulties; in the US and Saudi Arabia the term 'learning difficulties' is used for dyslexia while 'mental retardation' is used for more general learning difficulties. These types of terms lead towards a discrepancy model for assessing dyslexia; that is, there should be a discrepancy between general ability (usually seen as being measured through IQ) and ability in literacy.
- Making reasonable adjustments for examinations and to the learning environment. This builds on the social model of disability and requires an assessment to be made so that the social learning environment can be adjusted to allow learning to take place. The responsibility for the child's learning is placed firmly with the teacher, who must adapt approaches to teaching to ensure that the child learns. This can include the use of technological aids within the classroom and it can also include differentiated teaching (e.g. by increasing adult support, modifying the task, changing learning outcomes for a classroom task).
- Challenging teachers who may have become blasé about a child's learning based on their literacy performance. In this scenario, teachers note the child's low ability in literacy and assume that this is also true of their ability to learn other content. Consequently, work is given to the child that is well within their ability and does not stimulate further learning, either stymieing development or reducing motivation for school.

As was suggested at the end of the previous chapter on teaching reading, an informed knowledge of what we can do as educators to assist children who have what appears to be dyslexia is bound up with precise knowledge of a child's strengths and any areas for development. This involves careful identification of children with significant problems in their reading performance and subsequent thorough (or 'diagnostic') assessment for dyslexia, utilising a range of indicators which includes, but is not restricted to, reading.

- Identifying a learner's strengths so that they can maximise their assets and support learning. This can include informing learners about the ways that they seem to learn best and what strategies they can use to help themselves become more successful learners.
- Precisely identifying the literacy skills that have been mastered so that teaching of new skills can be matched to learning. The development of spelling skills has been shown to follow the same path for dyslexic pupils as for non-dyslexic pupils, but is slower (Treiman, 1997). This means that pupils with dyslexia have incomplete learning before the curriculum moves on for the majority of pupils in the class. With poor foundations, this makes the learning of more advanced spelling even harder. A good assessment enables the teacher to ensure that learning has been mastered and is not still at the acquisition stage before introducing new steps.

Q2 Are all pupils with dyslexia assessed?

Chapter 1 led us into the debate around what we mean by dyslexia, reflecting on the different uses of the term. There are numerous children who might be considered to be dyslexic at some point in their lives, many of whom will not receive a 'diagnosis'. Although some form of assessment may have been undertaken, it may not have been multiprofessional, thus undermining the validity of any conclusions. Equally, some children may be described as dyslexic who actually have some other difficulty because a differential diagnosis has not been undertaken.

There are limited human resources available to make multiprofessional assessments and this leads to political and arbitrary decisions being made about which children are assessed (Bond *et al.*, 2010). Inconsistent policy at local and national level has also been cited as a barrier to a fair assessment system (Reid, 2012). National bodies representing different pressure groups or professions also add to the debate about who should be allowed to assess and diagnose dyslexia, with arguments around the types of qualifications that render a person suitable. In some countries, states or districts there are also laws or rules that state how the assessment should be undertaken and what measures should be used to define dyslexia. In other countries, there are more relaxed approaches to assessment. This is not actually directly about the content of assessment but about the political, cultural and financial contexts *around* assessment (McDowell and O'Keeffe, 2012).

The differing reasons for the assessment and lack of communication between parties (learner, parents, teachers and other professionals involved in the assessment) can lead to those being assessed simply not understanding what has happened to them or what it means for them, raising a number of unsettling questions, including whether they are dyslexic. What does 'significant difficulties with reading' actually mean? If the result is 'negative', and a child is not dyslexic, then what exactly does this mean? Such a situation is hardly ideal from an ethical point of view or helpful in motivating learners to work on their personal areas for academic development (Armstrong and Humphrey, 2009).

Reflective questions

Think about the context in which you are working:

- Why is it important to know whether pupils are dyslexic or not?
- Are there conflicting demands that might require different types of assessment?
- Are there local or national regulations or laws that require specific types of assessment to be undertaken?
- Who would be involved in carrying out an assessment of dyslexia? If more than one person, what are their respective roles?

Specialist teachers and assessment for dyslexia

Traditionally, the assessment of dyslexia has been seen as complicated, involving a good understanding of psychology and psychometrics, and has been largely undertaken by qualified psychologists. However, there has been a persistent shortage of educational psychologists in the UK and this has acted as driver for increasing teacher skill in assessment of dyslexia (Armstrong and Squires, 2012; Atkinson and Squires, 2011). However, at the same time, there have been worries about the competencies of teachers to correctly differentiate dyslexia from other conditions that might also lead to poor reading or spelling progress. Since the late 1990s, in the UK and US, this has led to the development of specialist teachers who have undertaken further training in assessment and in dyslexia intervention. In the UK, at least, a key attribute of a specialist teacher has been suggested as the ability to conceptually understand and practically carry out diagnostic assessment for dyslexia (Bell, 2013; Klein, 1999; Rose, 2009).

There is some debate around how specialist assessment differs from assessment through teaching. Slow readers and slow spellers can be assessed by the classroom teacher by comparing the learning of each child with that of their peers. In Chapter 1, we discussed how there is a gradu-ated system of response to ensure that the slower learners are provided with more opportunities to learn. In the US, the ongoing assessment struc-ture of the response to intervention model (RTI) had been chosen by the majority of US states by 2010 (see Berkeley *et al.*, 2009; Hallahan *et al.*, 2012). RTI 'typically involves three tiers of progressively more intensive instruction' where Tier 1, at least, is administered by the non-specialist general classroom teacher (Hallahan *et al.*, 2012, p. 141). The assessment of reading and RTI share a history, indeed, with children who were at risk of reading failure as one of the main populations for which RTI was evolved (see Chapter 2, 'Some thoughts on teaching reading'). Whether a specialist teacher should be involved in Tier 2 and Tier 3 of an RTI model (or simply Tier 3) is an open question. There is also the more fundamental associated question as to whether RTI should, to some extent, replace a formal diagnostic assessment.

This is not a question that is restricted to readers of this book who live in the US and in Canada because, as was suggested in the earlier chapters, there is increasing international interest by policy-makers and education-alists in RTI (see also Frederickson and Cline, 2009). Some advocates of substantive change in the delivery of public services for children in Australia with disabilities have, for example, argued that RTI might be adopted across Australia because 'it does not require a diagnostic label' for initiation of support and funded services to affected children (McDowell and O'Keeffe, 2012). This proposal makes perfect sense, since children who are slow readers or poor spellers for any number of reasons, including dyslexia, need to have learning opportunities matched to their level of skill acquisition and delivered at a suitable pace to support further learning.

But there are several strong reasons why a discrete diagnostic assessment should not be replaced by RTI, however appealing RTI might appear and whatever merits it might have in other respects. Slow reading development and poor spelling skills can result from a number of different reasons – for example:

- Dyslexia.
- Specific language impairment, expressive and/or receptive language skills are impaired and this limits the extent to which a child can learn written language skills. The simple model of reading takes this into account (Rose, 2009).
- Attentional difficulties such as ADHD. The child cannot sustain atten-tion on the learning task or focus attention on the salient aspects of the learning task.

- General learning difficulties, developmental delay and mental retardation. These different labels all imply that the child is generally a slow learner and slow developer. Cognitive processes that underpin literacy development are not as well developed as they are in peers. This is likely to be evident in everything that the child does.
- Behavioural difficulties. The child is difficult to motivate or resists learning. The challenges presented to the teacher mean that the child misses learning opportunities.
- Hearing impairment. Even a low-level hearing impairment may mean that a child cannot hear all of the sounds that make up spoken words clearly and this makes it more difficult when it comes to learning synthetic phonics.

It is not surprising, therefore, that RTI is poor at identifying a specific learning difficulty, such as dyslexia. On the surface, the teacher sees poor reading or poor spelling compared to peers and adjusts teaching accordingly. But the observed behaviours or 'symptoms' do not fully explain the cause of the problem. Hallahan *et al.* (2012) make several persuasive points on this issue, pointing out that 'little research evidence exists regarding the effectiveness of RTI in identifying students with learning disabilities' and also that 'much of what we know about RTI is focused just on reading' (p. 141). As pointed out in Chapter 1, a clear finding from over 25 years of research in this area is that dyslexia, while demonstrably affecting an individual's reading, writing and spelling, has a range of often subtle but distinctive underpinning cognitive indicators which can affect many aspects of a student's learning and academic performance (Vellutino *et al.*, 2004).

This discussion has therefore already divulged the following about identification and assessment of dyslexia in individuals:

- Discrete diagnostic assessment has an important place on its own merit (although this does not imply anything – positive or negative – about RTI whatsoever: that is a separate issue).
- Irrespective of issues around the cultural, ethical or financial implications of a diagnosis, such as gatekeeping access to funded services, a discrete and thorough assessment is required on purely diagnostic grounds to accurately detect the possible presence of dyslexia.
- Diagnostic assessment should contain more than an assessment of reading and spelling; it should also identify whether and to what extent there is the presence (or signature) of underpinning cognitive indicators consistent with dyslexia.

This last point has important implications for any consideration of what a specialist teacher should know (their knowledge base) and their consequent practice. This is because the idea of assessing a learner's cognitive functioning in areas such as working memory or IQ implies the use (and understanding of) standardised, psychometric tests. This endeavour also presupposes that working memory and IQ are accurately understood as scientific, technical concepts.

Across the developed world, at least, such knowledge has usually been the domain of psychologists (typically educational psychologists or clinical psychologists). These have typically completed an undergraduate degree in psychology; a postgraduate specialist qualification; and are usually registered with a professional body which regulates this professional field, including access to certain psychometric tests (APS, 2007; BPS, 2009). Internationally, it has not been common custom and practice for teachers to use or understand standardised, psychometric tests such as those necessary for a rigorous diagnostic assessment; nor have educators been expected, historically, to be able to interpret any resulting standardised data and arrive at probable conclusions. Such expectations are novel for the teaching profession.

Reflective questions

Are there specialist teachers in the context in which you are working? If so:

- What additional qualifications, training or experience do they have compared to non-specialist teachers?
- How do they support the teaching that takes place in the mainstream classroom?
- How is diagnostic assessment linked to assessment through teaching?

Should educators assess children, young people or adults for dyslexia? The assessment debate

As Bell (2013) points out in a recent study of teachers undertaking specialist training to assess and support children with dyslexia, the knowledge and skills inherent in this pose a considerable (practical and intellectual) challenge for participating teachers (p. 13). This creates a potential dilemma about whether educators should assess for dyslexia or whether this should remain a role for other professionals. In a measured response to this dilemma it is helpful to consider the fundamental question as to whether educators should be involved in assessing learners for dyslexia, particularly children and young people. It is highly valuable for practitioners, decision-makers in settings and educational institutions themselves to pause and carefully consider this question before setting out commitments in policy or in practice. There are implications at several connected levels for educators in assessing individuals for dyslexia.

Disciplinary: To what extent should teachers be involved in using psychological tools, practices and approaches often used primarily by psychologists? Is this actually warranted or an unhelpful extension of practice for educators whose focus should be classroom-based and directly related to teaching and learning? Are there any ethical implications associated with educators being involved in this province of practice? Will teachers understand the theoretical basis for the psychometric tools that they use?

Knowledge-based: Do educators have the knowledge base and sufficient conceptual understanding to, for example, select, use and interpret appropriate standardised, data-gathering tools? Will they know what makes a good tool? Will they know how to use tools together to form a holistic interpretation and generate hypotheses to support teaching and learning? Will they understand the concepts of psychometrics, such as standard error of measurement, reliability, testing frequency, confidence limits?

Pragmatic: Do educators have access to resources required (standardised assessments, for example, cost several hundred US dollars at the time of publication), particularly when several might be needed? Do educators have access to initial professional learning and, most importantly, regular professional updates around assessment? Will the test publishers trust teachers and sell them the tests they want to use? Can teachers make better use of other information that is already available in schools to help in the assessment of a child?

Philosophical and ethical: What (professional) safeguards are there to ensure that data is gathered appropriately/sensitively and interpreted in an accurate, meaningful way? Should psychometric tests be used at all with children, young people and adults in education? Are their particular risks and responsibilities inherent in assessing children and young people classed as minors? Do teachers understand the need for confidentiality? Are there mechanisms in place to ensure that tests are kept secure?

One critical observation which might be made of education systems across the English-speaking world is that there is a tendency for new ideas to be enthusiastically embraced by education policy-makers, schools or college leaders and also, often, educators themselves. There are, of course, positive dimensions to being constructively open to change, but there are, it should be said, also disadvantages.

One problematic assumption often made in this quest for 'the new' is that change is, of itself, intrinsically positive in its effects. An associated problem is a lack of careful consideration as to whether practices which are *possible* are actually, on balance, probably *beneficial* too. Without straying too far into philosophical territory, there are many actions which are possible; many of them would, however, not be wise to recommend and often for reasons which are more subtle or complex than are immediately obvious on first inspection.

Indeed, one important criticism often made of educational policy in some parts of the English-speaking world (and elsewhere) is that it is premised upon often incautious and politically driven 'change agenda' as opposed to a carefully reasoned, long-term view of what is most probably beneficial for students and educators. Policy from this critical angle is flavoured by the political demands of each 24-hour news-cycle and facile knee-jerk behaviourism promoted by trivialising social media.

In their excellent edited book *Bad Education: Debunking Myths in Education,* Adey and Dillon (2012), for example, comment critically on the sheer quantity of policy directed at teachers, commenting: 'Over the last 25 years teachers have been subject to an increasing barrage of instructions, advice and statutory regulation, all designed by an administration that acts as if the fine details of classroom life can be fully controlled' (p. xxiii).

These problems are not insurmountable and there are training packages with accreditation open to teachers. It is not currently clear whether asking educators to expand their role into psychological assessment is unwise or, alternatively, progressive and forward thinking. In this book, our role is not to direct readers towards conclusions but instead to offer opportunities for deeper consideration so that decisions about practice are better informed.

Pre-assessment questions: the value of a pre-assessment process

One possible helpful strategy here is to reconsider specialist assessment in a more nuanced way, invoking a set of critical questions which can inform a decision-making process and better respond to this complex issue. Core critical questions to be asked pre-assessment by specialist teachers could include:

- What do we already know about this individual?
- What value will any further assessment add?
- Who needs the assessment and for what purpose?

- Are there any drawbacks to carrying out a specialist assessment with this individual and any foreseeable adverse impacts?
- From what is already known about this individual, is further assessment best done by another specialist or specialists?

In the context of identification of a child's possible difficulties, Frederickson and Cline (2009, p. 133) make three highly pragmatic suggestions which 'have received wide support and are important well beyond the identification stage'. These are:

Parents must be fully involved throughout. For young people under the age of 18, full involvement of parents from the outset will add a crucial dimension to the picture, including vital context to other information gathered. Once young people reach adulthood, this is more complex and depends a lot on the culture in which the young person lives. In the UK, the assessment for young adults is likely to be done with the adult and not involve their parents. In contrast, parents in Malta are very keen to be involved even when their child is completing a degree.

Everyone who knows the child must collaborate. Errors will be minimised when there is close co-operation and communication between any health and social service professional who knows a child and the teachers who have responsibility for him or her in school. If views from different perspective are sought, listened to and reconciled, it is less likely that the child's difficulties will be misunderstood because of one person's (or one profession's) blind spot. More importantly, multiple sources of evidence can be combined to provide a holistic view of the child's difficulties.

Intervention should have a low profile. Low-profile helping strategies will build on the normal school routine of the child's class group. The effect will be to reduce any potentially stigmatising effects of labelling to a minimum.

Reflective questions

- To what extent should assessment be carried out by specialists?
- What contribution can general teachers make to the assessment process?
- Why is it important to involve parents of school-age children in the assessment process?

The assessment process and labelling: process led rather than event led

The labelling of a child or young person as 'dyslexic' is a key outcome of any assessment and leads to decisions about teaching and provision. It is also an event which will potentially register across an individual's life, with significant personal implications. Even for adults, the confirmation or discovery that they probably have dyslexia can set off a causal chain of introspection and carry a major emotional charge – for example, 'All those years thinking I was stupid'; 'I always wondered why study was so difficult' (Alexander-Passe, 2012; Riddick, 2010).

In a highly pertinent discussion about labelling of children and young people with a disability and its relationship with assessment, Riddick (2012, p. 29) helpfully suggests a list of advantages and disadvantages to such labelling. Riddick (2012) also emphasises the value of a more nuanced, less black and white approach to the labelling process which sensitively monitors how labels are 'operationalised' over time. As she suggests, this is a potentially complex task involving multiple dimensions of monitoring by an educator.

This sounds like a simple undertaking but actually a range of variables have to be taken into account, including the context of the labelling; pre-existing beliefs about the term for all concerned; the age of the child; how the label has been negotiated and over what period of time; what actions and attitudes the label has led to both in school and in the wider community; how it has impacted on a child's educational performance, their social interactions and self-efficacy as a learner (p. 33). A logical extension of Riddick's suggestion is that monitoring the effects of assessment over time on a student is itself construed as an intrinsic, key part of the assessment process.

This view discloses that parts of the assessment process (particularly monitoring the effects of labelling) will carry on over months and even years rather than being dominated by a single data-gathering event involving the use of a structured interview and psychometric tests, followed by a written report. A further implication is that the involved professional, whether a specialist teacher or psychologist, has a longer-term relationship with the child/young person and potentially his/her family, enabling them to do this.

A small but growing strand of research involving individuals with dyslexia supports the need for a more meaningful experience of assessment. For many of those affected, this research suggests, dyslexia is something they meaningfully understand months or years *after* the assessment takes place and after talking to friends or family (Alexander-Passe, 2012; Armstrong and Humphrey, 2009; Riddick, 2010). This unsatisfactory situation discloses how (ethically and professionally) important it is for clear, explicit communication with the individual at the time of assessment about what is happening and what this might mean for their life.

In many cases (particularly for younger children) it is important that family/carers are party to these explanations and can accurately revisit them in future. This is discussed in more detail later in this chapter. One important implication of this approach to practice is that professionals involved in diagnostic assessment, specifically a specialist teacher, should cultivate a professional but friendly and open relationship with the individual and their carers/family. This not only aids communication with the family but has pragmatic benefits: many tests involving performance, which might form part of a wider diagnostic assessment, assume that test anxiety is not a complicating factor (Putwain and Daniels, 2010; von der Embse *et al.*, 2013).

Ethically, it is very important that the individual involved does not suffer undue anxiety as a result of assessment; professionals involved have a strong duty of care to ensure that any potential causes of anxiety are minimised if at all possible. This is enshrined internationally in the sections of professional conduct codes dealing with assessment and in established professional organisations such as the British Psychological Society (BPS, 2009) and Australian Psychological Society (APS, 2007). The APS Code of Ethics has explicit sections on assessment which link with its emphasis upon the prevention of harm and responsibility for conduct. These are bracketed under 'Professional responsibility'.

B.3. Professional responsibility

Psychologists provide *psychological services* in a responsible manner. Having regard to the nature of the *psychological services* they are providing, *psychologists*:

(a) act with the care and skill expected of a competent psychologist;
(b) take responsibility for the reasonably foreseeable consequences of their *conduct*;
(c) take reasonable steps to prevent harm occurring as a result of their *conduct*.

(APS, 2007, p. 20, emphases original)

A friendly professional who clearly explains what will come next and scaffolds assessment procedure can aid this ethical imperative in terms of mitigating any possible harm. It should also be stated that taking part in a diagnostic assessment should, for ethical reasons, always be voluntary and done with an individual's informed consent. This cannot be gained without clear pre-assessment information on what the assessment will contain and what it seeks to understand or look for. This might have to be appropriately phrased with younger children or where an issue affecting communication/understanding is suspected.

In our experience, the following can be a non-threatening but accessible general summary to communicate to individuals pre-assessment, offering an example of what we might say. In our script we do not mention dyslexia because our assessment might lead us to think there are no major difficulties or there is a different underlying condition.

> I'd like to work with you today to explore what you are good at and what you are not so good at and to help you think about what helps you to learn. This will involve getting you to write and read, and also looking at other things which might affect your learning. It will take a whole morning or whole afternoon to do. Afterwards, we will talk about how you did and think about what this means and how you and your teachers can help you learn. It might be that you are working well in some areas and less well in others. I have been asked to write a report for your parents and teachers so that they know how well you have done. When we talk later, I will tell you the kinds of things that I will be saying and some ideas that I have about how you learn best.
>
> Is it okay for us to work together? If you are sure that you don't want this to happen, then that's fine too. Just let me know.

It should also be stated that there is no value in assuming a pseudo-objective approach to diagnostic assessment in our behaviours; this is sometimes done because it is (falsely) perceived as 'clinical' and, therefore, more suited to the needs of assessment objectivity. To offer a contrary perspective, in any diagnostic assessment we are investigating the possibility that this unique human individual might have a thing that we refer to as dyslexia. Humanising them and our interactions with them, within a professional framework, can help us appreciate dimensions which can have a bearing on this question. Indeed, in our experience, individuals are more likely to be open and honest in their interactions with us if we are open and honest with them in our interactional style: they imitate our behaviours. Several theories for behavioural science, cognitive psychology and cognitive psychology support this observation, including, for example, the influential mirror neuron hypothesis (Iacoboni, 2009).

It is also worth noting that, in this book, the term 'diagnostic assessment' is used rather than 'dyslexia assessment'. This is for two reasons:

1   **Philosophical:** we need to be open to what the data we gather suggests rather than approach assessment looking for dyslexia – or looking to disprove this individual might have it.
2   **Pragmatic:** in many cases a thorough diagnostic assessment will suggest that the person is, on balance, unlikely to have dyslexia, but will often highlight *other* significant issues affecting their learning. These can vary widely in my experience: from a possible mental health problem

to evidence of hearing (sensory) impairments. In such cases the best option is always referral to other relevant specialists. Even the most capable practitioner will, from time to time, also encounter unusual cases which defy classification: these call for a second opinion from a trusted colleague and additional careful, open-minded consideration. In other cases, data gathered suggests that the person, on balance, probably has dyslexia, but it also suggests that this co-exists with other issues which require assessment by other specialists.

The discrepancy model: should we – shouldn't we?

There has been a debate in recent years about the use of the discrepancy model for diagnosing dyslexia. Partly, this has been led by the BPS working party definition of dyslexia which reviewed the literature and came to the view that, from a teaching perspective, the model does not make much sense and by itself cannot diagnose dyslexia. In this section, we are going to cover the basic ideas behind the model and explore some of the critiques of it by researchers, practitioners and scholars.

Using an intelligence test to simply provide a unitary score is not very informative and it does not explain much in terms of dyslexia; it only predicts how likely a child is to succeed at school. Some children with low IQs can do particularly well if the teaching is right and they are well motivated. The discrepancy model is based on the idea that there is an underlying general cognitive factor, which Spearman called g, which, for most people, indicates that all areas of cognitive ability are roughly the same. Any differences between scores can be compared to see how unusual such a difference is in the population and whether such a difference would be expected to occur by chance. The analysis which is carried out is an ipsative analysis and compares one area of performance with another to identify a person's relative strengths and relative weaknesses. Typical analyses allow the following comparisons:

- **Cluster scores on the intelligence battery**. Intelligence tests produce several different types of scores and subtests are clustered around factors which are linked to neurological models of cognitive processing. For instance, discrepancy analysis will allow exploration of whether visual scores are higher than verbal scores or vice versa; whether there is a weakness in working memory or in speed of processing. On some tests, such as the Wechsler Individual Achievement Test (WIAT), a comparison can be made between General Conceptual Ability, the Full Scale IQ score and the Cognitive Flexibility Index. In Chapter 1, we discussed several theories about the causation of dyslexia; a weakness

in working memory or speed of processing *could* be indicative of dyslexia. We also pointed out that these weaknesses could be indicators
of other types of difficulties such as dyspraxia or ADHD.
- **Subtest scores within a cluster.** This is useful for generating hypotheses
  about the sub-processes involved in solving the different types of problems. Each subtest draws upon a range of cognitive processes and a
  comparison allows the tester to come up with a set of hunches that
  might explain why the testee is struggling with some aspect of learning. Strategies can then be suggested to improve academic support and
  for self-help or alternative ways of learning.

Discrepancy analysis is useful and allows the generation of hypotheses
which can then be explored through further assessment. This can include
functional analysis of learning; dynamic assessment; curriculum-based
assessment; assessment through teaching; and learning by trying out particular approaches through experiments or programmes of intervention.

There is another use for discrepancy analysis that is more controversial.
The model has been extended to compare cognitive ability with attainments because there is a correlation between both sets of scores. A person
with high general ability *usually* scores well on tests of literacy. In this
approach the tester uses the cognitive ability of the testee to predict what
they would achieve on the attainment tests. They then compare the actual
score with the predicted score. Differences occur anyway because the two
scores are not perfectly correlated in the general population. The tester
then looks to see if the size of the difference is unusual and not produced
by chance. This allows the tester to say whether absolute poor performance (i.e. compared to other people of the same age) on a test of literacy
is also relative poor performance (ipsative comparison) for the individual
being tested. The argument goes that if the testee has low intelligence then
this can explain low absolute performance on the literacy tests. It allows
the tester to say whether the poor literacy score is due to a general learning
difficulty or to a specific learning difficulty. In some places in the world,
this discrimination between general or specific leads to the allocation of
resources or not and, consequently, the use of discrepancy testing has been
written into policy documents and laws.

The approach can be criticised for a number of reasons:

- When we think about children who are learning to read, we know that
  dyslexic children learn to read more slowly than generally poor readers, but in the same way (Treiman, 1997). This means that younger
  children or those with developmental delays or with general learning
  difficulties would respond to the same kinds of teaching. If the same

kind of teaching leads to the same outcome, irrespective of the discrepancy, then surely there should be equal access to the teaching programmes. This raises questions about the use of discrepancy models in making policy decisions regarding resource allocation. To get around this problem, the BPS working party provided a definition of dyslexia that simply involved knowing that the child had been struggling with reading for a long time, despite appropriate teaching.

- A discrepancy between general cognitive ability and attainment can occur for a variety of reasons. For instance, the testee may have missed a lot of schooling and crucial learning; they may be poorly motivated and missing crucial learning; they may have a specific language impairment; they may have poor attentional control skills; they may be dyslexic; etc. A single psychometric assessment that only considers scores produced cannot discriminate between the different possibilities. This means that a discrepancy by itself cannot be used to diagnose dyslexia. The discrepancy can contribute to a holistic assessment in which ipsative cognitive scores are used to support the diagnosis alongside clinical observation made during testing and diagnostic interviewing. Further support can come from naturalistic observation of the learner in the learning environment and from assessment through teaching.
- For people with low cognitive ability, there is not much scope for variation between scores and this means that a discrepancy is less likely when general learning difficulties are apparent. This means that if a discrepancy model is used, only the primary difficulty of general learning difficulties (or moderate learning difficulties) is likely to be diagnosed. The intervention that follows is more likely to cover the whole curriculum, either through differentiation, adaptation or a different educational placement. It could be argued that if a wider intervention is used it will also cover literacy development. However, it might also restrict access to particular literacy interventions when local or national policies require a discrepancy in order to access these programmes or supports.

Should we throw the baby out with the bath water and abandon the discrepancy model altogether? We suggest not and for two important reasons. First, a discrepancy between low literacy scores and higher cognitive scores is useful for other purposes. It allows teachers to understand that the learner is more able cognitively than they might have imagined by looking at their written work. This sets a challenge to teachers to provide academically demanding work while at the same time supporting access to the work and supporting the recording of ideas. Second, if the discrepancy model is used in a way to generate hypotheses about the learner, then other assessment data can be used to explore these hypotheses. Only when all of the available data has been considered can the diagnosis of dyslexia be made.

A good use of discrepancy analyses would involve an understanding of both the current theories about the causation of dyslexia and neuropsychological models about information processing from cognitive psychology:

- Compare the main factor scores from the test battery being used (e.g. Full Scale IQ with General Ability Index with Cognitive Flexibility Index);
- Compare cluster scores within each factor (e.g. within General Ability Index compare verbal comprehension with perceptual reasoning).
- Compare subtest scores within each cluster (e.g. within verbal comprehension compare similarities with vocabulary).
- For each comparison, state the confidence limits and unusualness of each discrepancy in the wider population.
- Use the underlying theory through which the test battery was designed (e.g. Cattell–Horn–Carroll theory) to generate hypotheses about underlying cognitive processes and comparing this to theories about the causation of dyslexia.
- Note clinical observations made at the time of testing and use these to explore hypotheses generated. Further support this through clinical interviews which include reflection on cognitive processes and their impact on daily living.
- Use the most appropriate factor score to predict attainment subtest scores on a co-normed test and then compare these to actual scores. State confidence limits and unusualness.
- Support the hypothesis of a specific difficulty through functional analysis of errors made during the literacy assessment. Link this back to theories about dyslexia.
- If possible carry out further assessments to explore the hypotheses generated (e.g. test phonological awareness, use assessment through teaching approaches).
- Make sure that any comparisons between the individual being tested and the wider population are made with the correct peer group: school pupils with school pupils of the same age and culture; university students with other undergraduates.
- Look at the whole pattern and all of the data to make a holistic decision about whether this particular assessment leads to the conclusion that a diagnosis of dyslexia is appropriate.

Reflective questions

- How useful is IQ testing as part of the assessment process?
- Why is a discrepancy alone not a good way to identify dyslexia?
- What positive aspects are there to looking for discrepancies?
- In what ways can discrepancy analysis be helpful to the identification process? Is it just about labels?

Assessment revisited: some protocols

It is convenient to perceive any specialist diagnostic assessment as being primarily a challenge concerning knowledge – for example, educators grappling with the principles of psychometric assessment. In reality, the actual content of any assessment (what subtests are used and why) is relatively straightforward. It is the issues before, around and after assessment which are, in many ways, more challenging to respond to and require more careful consideration in approach. It is, therefore, worth summarising the key points in thinking about protocols that might be developed.

First, we have to consider the purpose of the assessment. If it is part of a bureaucratic process simply to allocate resources then we have to play by the rules of that decision-making process, even if we know that it has its flaws and may not be ideal. Such systems usually specify what is needed and have an underlying principle of fairness of access to the resources. The people who designed the system will have some basis for arguing that they want an accurate diagnosis of dyslexia, but they may provide a limited way of exploring the available evidence and may constrain the use of some types of evidence in favour of others. This is important to realise, since a diagnosis of dyslexia may be given if the assessment is done for some other purpose, but resources may not be allocated if the evidence provided does not conform to the rubric required for resource allocation decisions.

Second, if diagnosis is about improving teaching then we might ask whether a diagnosis is really necessary. Teachers should be flexible in their approach and follow Vygostkian principles to match teaching to learning. This is the principle underpinning philosophies such as the inclusion movement, RTI and social models of disability.

Third, we need to be conscious of some of the socio-political pressures that act upon teachers and parents and may cause anxiety for both. Assessments that deal with this will need to consider how the pupil compares to peers of the same age and be sensitive enough to identify whether a child is in the average range, mildly below average or has a severe difficulty.

Fourth, it is preferable to carry out the assessment in a way that makes use of a wide range of information sources and builds up over time. When this is not possible then a discrete psychometric assessment can be used to give a person's performance on a given day, within specified levels of confidence (usually 90–95 per cent confidence limits). We can be more confident in a diagnosis when multiple sources of data help us reach the same conclusion.

Our view is that assessment can take many forms and there is significant value in an assessment process which critically asks a set of questions and can inform subsequent decisions about whether or not to carry out a psychometric assessment. Data already known about this individual, garnered from other professionals/the individuals' family can be helpfully used here. This leads us to some possible starting points and key questions to ask.

1   Is the difficulty in the area of reading, spelling or writing? Or is it a more general difficulty? That is, can we differentiate between a specific learning difficulty that might be dyslexia or a moderate learning difficulty or a global developmental delay? This part of the assessment can draw upon a whole range of information sources – for example:

   (a) general development and self-help skills, including parental history of developmental milestones;
   (b) patterns of performance across the curriculum using teacher assessments, external assessments of learning and pre-school assessment history. Perhaps there are some areas of the curriculum in which the learner excels while they struggle in those requiring literacy;
   (c) teacher observations of differences in oral ability compared to written ability (e.g. the pupil is good at answering questions in class but never gets anything down on paper);
   (d) social skills and non-academic interaction with peers as an indicator of general maturity.

2   Could there be a sensory impairment? Can the child see well and hear well? Classroom observations might include noting if the child can respond to varying intensities of sound or checking visual pattern matching. Other clues might come from looking at drawings or seeing what the child notices in their environment. More formal hearing checks need to be more than a test of whether the child can hear. An audiogram can indicate mild hearing loss at particular frequencies that would make it difficult for the child to hear and distinguish between similar phonemes. This makes it difficult to put sounds to letter patterns. Sight tests need to check vision, stereoscopic vision and ocular stability. If a clear stable image is not being detected by both eyes then it is more difficult to match letter shape to sound.

3   Could there be an underlying language problem? Expressive and receptive language skills underpin reading and writing. If the child has a specific language impairment, then they may not understand the text. Part of the assessment could include:

(a) checking understanding of spoken instructions;
(b) checking verbal ability;
(c) making use of curriculum-based assessments of language skills, such as the Foundation Profile in England;
(d) observing and listening to spoken language in the classroom and playground as it occurs during natural conversations. Is it grammatically correct (for the age group)? Are the spoken words clear? Do the responses match the language produced by the other child? Are attentional skills and social interaction skills good?
(e) having a screening test performed by a speech and language therapist.

If the answers to the above questions are continuing to suggest that the learner's difficulties are dyslexia, then a psychometric assessment can add to the assessment that has already been undertaken. A diagnostic assessment should contain more than an assessment of reading and spelling: it should also identify whether and to what extent there is the presence (or signature) of underpinning cognitive indicators consistent with the main cognitive psychology theories of dyslexia. In line with some of the points already raised in this chapter and Chapter 1 there is a need to consider the following:

• The assessment needs to be sensitive to the cultural, ethical and financial context in which the assessment is undertaken. Again, this has to be linked to the purpose of the assessment.
• Consideration needs to be given to the comparator group of peers. It is one thing to compare seven year olds with other seven-year-old children, but quite a different thing to compare university students with all adults of the same age.
• How are the results of the psychometric assessment to be reported? We saw in Chapter 1 that age-equivalent scores are confusing when people do not realise that half of the age group score below their age level. Centiles are rank order positions; again many people worry that 16 centile may be the bottom of the average range but it seems a long way from 50 centile. This is a misconception, the distance between centile points in real performance terms is very great at the extremes (1 and 2 centile, or 99 and 100 centile) and less so in the middle of the scale. Standard scores refer to performance levels, but are hard for

most people to understand. Perhaps a better way of reporting scores is simply to use broad descriptors such as:

- o   well below average (−2 standard deviations or worse);
- o   below average (−1 to −2 standard deviations);
- o   average (−1 to +1 standard deviations);
- o   above average (+1 to +2 standard deviations).

David McLoughlin asks report authors to consider the potential uses of test reports, particularly for adults. He suggests that reports could be sectioned so that the person who has been tested can decide whether to give employers or university staff a summary; a more detailed but descriptive interpretative report with recommendations and technical adjustments; or the full report, including a technical appendix. He also suggests using more positive language and replacing terms such as 'below average' with weak; 'average' with competent; and, 'above average' with good (McLoughlin, 2012). While this might be useful in terms of making reasonable adjustments to study, examinations or workplaces, it may prove unhelpful if the report is being used for bureaucratic purposes such as the allocation of funding. The language used may, therefore, reflect the potential purposes for which the report will be used.

- Psychometric assessment reports need to identify relative strengths as well as weaknesses. They should comment on both absolute scores (comparing the individual to peers) and also on ipsative scores (comparing the individual to themselves).
- There are significant questions for educational managers and institutions which should inform whether practitioners and institutions offer diagnostic assessment by a specialist educator or, for example, commission external specialists/other providers (such as private psychologists) to provide this service for the setting. These questions are pragmatic but also disciplinary and knowledge-based.

Differential assessment may lead to the application of one or more labels. Labelling is a key factor to consider before, during and post assessment. Indeed, monitoring the effects of assessment over time on a student should be construed as an intrinsic key part of the assessment process rather than as something separate. What are the emotional impacts of diagnosis? How does the learner respond to changes made to their learning programme? Do they learn more effectively after the diagnosis and in response to the environmental and teaching changes that are made?

Assessment should be ethically sound and, as such, should be with the informed consent of the learner and their family, if they are a child. Clear, appropriate information affecting any decisions arising from the assessment should be given at every stage so that children and adults can be involved in the decision process. This also means sharing the implications of the assessment on learning, resource allocation, adjustments to the learning environment, the use of technology and opportunities for the future.

Reflective questions

In the context in which you work, write an assessment protocol based on the ideas in Chapter 1 and Chapter 3. Think about:

- the purpose of the assessment;
- the teaching and learning context;
- types of evidence and data that could be used to inform the assessment;
- any restrictions on what counts as acceptable evidence and the limitations that this might impose upon diagnosis of dyslexia;
- ethical issues;
- any key points for reporting the outcomes of assessments.

Chapter 4

Dyslexia and behaviour

Introduction: the enduring appeal of behaviour

The behaviour of children and young people in educational settings is an enduring issue which regularly arouses controversy. Concerns about the behaviour of children and young people with SEND have particularly shaped educational policy and practice in the UK, US, Australia and elsewhere since compulsory schooling began (DCSF, 2009a; DfES, 2004, 2005b, 2007; HMSO, 1989; OFSTED, 2005; Squires, 2012; Steer, 2009; US Department of Education, 2004). In parallel, researchers, teachers, parents and influential organisations – for example, the British Dyslexia Association (BDA) in the UK and the Australian Federation of SPELD Associations (AUSPELD) in Australia – have placed new or renewed emphasis upon the importance of behavioural factors in the learning, development and welfare of children described as having dyslexia (see Introduction). Philosophically, if we consider the idea that dyslexia is a cultural label for a wide range of what society describes as 'difficulties' arising from the interactions between the bio-psycho-social dimensions of an individual (see Chapter 1), then we might also reflect that the social circumstances in which dyslexia is mentioned by teachers or by those affected is likely, is some small way, to affect a child's perceptions, judgements and subsequent actions. Behaviour here could be seen as a potentially integral part of the phenomenon we describe as dyslexia – rather than as something 'out there' and separate.

This is not, however, what is being usually referred to when 'behaviour' is mentioned by education policy, by politicians in the media, in schools or by parents or teachers. 'Behaviour', here, is synonymous with 'poor' behaviour which threatens educational standards (DfE, 2010) or is presented as evidence of a decline in the moral standards of children and young people (Petley *et al.*, 2013). For children in the UK there is even an important formal label: social, emotional and behavioural difficulties (SEBD). This recognises substantive, enduring problems in social, emotional and behavioural areas of a child's development. In Australia, the

US, Canada and elsewhere, the similar (though slightly different) term 'emotional and behavioural difficulties' (EBD) is often used (Armstrong, 2013).

What follows disentangles this important topic for the reader, identifying some implications for the care, development and educational success of learners with dyslexia. In keeping with the critical perspective of this book, this topic is explored in terms of the behaviours of teachers and other adults in a child's life, as well as the child or young person. Indeed, I make the suggestion that 'relationships' should be substituted for 'behaviours' within practice and outline the merits of this shift. This chapter also explores the important shared ground between dyslexia, SEBD and EBD. This is a key relationship which is re-examined in the book's conclusion.

Thinking critically about behaviour

It is important to note that this chapter is not a 'how to' guide to the everyday classroom management of children with or without SEND. Indeed, we might be sceptical whether any 'how to' approach can work for all teachers and all children in all situations. I do offer key recommendations for educational practice in relation to behaviour and dyslexia in this chapter's summary, but these are intended to provoke personal-professional reflection on this topic rather than as 'how to' behaviour management guide. Further, highly accessible resources in this area are also signposted for the reader, such as the Hanbury's excellent book with ideas for children with autism that can be readily used with pupils who are dyslexic (Hanbury, 2012). Attention is given to some of the possible dimensions that educators might consider on this topic, including, for example, considering our own reactions to the behaviour of others and the relationships between behaviour and a child's developing self-system.

There are many ways of thinking about behaviour and the more reading around the topic that we can do, then the more able we are to understand the behaviour of others – with a greater repertoire of possible ways of acting (or reacting) in a proportional, calm and informed way. This might be thought of as encouraging insight into our behaviours in response to those of our students: what follows is intended to support and scaffold this process of critical self-awareness for the reader.

Alongside what is proposed as a helpful personal, intellectual process for educators run wider cultural and social processes which pattern the kind of decisions, actions and behaviours available to us: we might be professional individuals, but we work in educational institutions, governed, for example, by legislation. Despite what politicians may occasionally suggest, cultural and social factors outside the school gates cannot be ignored in terms of affecting pupil behaviours. As educators, we are subjected to the ideology, dogma and philosophical positioning of our culture as it is transmitted by the media. This impacts on the way that we view behaviour and influences our approaches to behaviour management. This also hold true for children and young people, who might react inappropriately or immaturely to the stresses they experience on account of imperfections in the education system, family problems or a multitude of other life stressors (Noble and McGrath, 2008). The social context is vital to note in understanding behaviour and in avoiding the (too convenient) perception that behaviour is solely down to the individual (a professional, a parent or a learner). Research over the last 25 years has, instead, cumulatively suggested that there are (socially, culturally) structural patterns in the associations between dyslexia and behaviour.

Dyslexia and wellbeing

In Chapter 1, we highlighted that there have been many neurological, medical and positivist studies about dyslexia that are concerned with causality (Vellutino et al., 2004). The medical model places the dyslexic difficulties firmly within the learners' physical makeup in common with others forms of SEN (Riddick, 2001, 2012). The individual with dyslexia is described within a medical model framework which calls on identification of 'symptoms' and other concepts which, often inadequately, describe them as 'suffering' from a form of disease and thereby diminishing their educational performance in relation to typically developing peers. Many researchers, writers and educationalists reserve particular criticism for this perspective on disability, stressing that it can reinforce an already existing negative, deficit-driven view of children with specific learning difficulties or other forms of SEND (Cooper, 2008; Wearmouth et al., 2003). While the reader, on reflection, may or may not agree with such criticisms, it is worth reflecting that many conditions are defined in this way in our society, using clinical criteria for assessment. This is often linked to the allocation of resources, interventions, treatments or specialist programmes (see Chapter 3). This is at odds with an inclusive education system in which all children are seen as different and individual. We might disagree with a medical view of disability, but it has proved stubbornly difficult to erase within education and related professions (Riddick, 2012).

One response to this wide-ranging debate about how to conceptualise dyslexia in relation to behaviours has been to sidestep the question of its biological origins altogether and, instead, suggest that what actually matters is the effect that an individual's educational difficulties have on their wellbeing: on them socially, psychologically, intellectually or behaviourally. A small but growing strand within research about dyslexia has also, explicitly or implicitly, adopted this view of behaviour (Armstrong and Humphrey, 2009; Burden, 2005; Burden and Burdett, 2005, 2007). Some researchers have gone so far as to suggest that the cultural, systemic inflexibility of education systems in the UK, US, Australia and elsewhere underlie these 'difficulties' experienced by children with SEND in their everyday study and behaviours – with predictably negative effects on their wellbeing (Cooper, 2008).

This might be categorised as owing something to a pragmatic-interactionist perspective. 'Pragmatic' because the question of biological causes of dyslexia are put to one side, suggesting that there is no certainty in exactly what parts of a child's behaviours are due to biologically based aspects of dyslexia. 'Interactionist' because the focus is instead on the way in which a child's behaviours are part of *their* interpretation of the human world – their 'meaning making' derived from personal everyday social experience and interaction with others (Ritzer, 2000). Research seeks to explore how wider socially or culturally based structural factors in education (education policy, the curriculum, content of teacher training, practice around diagnostic labelling) trickle down into the fine grain of daily experience for a child with SEND, at school or at home or both.

An advantage of a pragmatic-interactionist perspective, for educators, parents and children affected, particularly when compared with any approach informed by a deficit/medical model, is that it allows for *positive change*. Because the behaviours of children affected are seen as an evolving reaction to everyday experiences, this leaves the way open to alter a child's response through positive action by educators and schools. The Dyslexia Friendly School initiative in the UK can be seen in this light, particularly where it stresses the use of positive language around dyslexia and the need for positive, non-judgemental interactions by all adults in a setting with children.

For a specialist practitioner, it is *always* important to consider a learner's social and emotional wellbeing, whether we explicitly frame this in a specific theory or not. Attention to the wider welfare of children can also be rationalised:

- Through reference to legislation at state or national level; in the UK for example, *Every Child Matters* (DfES, 2004); and in the US under mandated IDEA (2004, 2009) legislation.
- On pragmatic grounds: educational interventions are surely more likely to succeed if a young person is free from substantial emotional disturbance.

- Fundamentally, attention to a learner's social and emotional state is wholly legitimate on moral grounds: we want that child to have a happy, productive, well-adjusted adulthood. This central moral outcome is also something that the UK, Australia and many other countries are legally committed to enabling for all children (UNESCO, 1994a, 1994b, 2000).

Dyslexia, SEND and educational outcomes: grounds for realism

Research exploring the social, emotional and psychological effect of dyslexia suggests that many individuals do not have a positive or productive experience of education, with negative consequences for later adulthood. Negative life outcomes for adults with dyslexia identified by research include, for example: unemployment; negative attitudes towards education; and even poor personal relationships (Burden, 2008). This suggests that, for many children with literacy difficulties, there are major educational barriers to achieving the positive future enjoyed by many of their non-dyslexic peers (Ainscow and Miles, 2008).

This is highly pertinent for a specialist teacher, alerting us to the realistic scale of the challenge we potentially face in everyday educational practice and in ensuring that learners under our care are not negatively affected by their increased risk of such poor outcomes. The realism inherent in this view can be a very helpful psychological frame for educators: it is not necessarily 'poor' teaching (or lack of effort, engagement or aptitude by our students) which is the root of the severe difficulties with study which some, if not most, children with dyslexia face. Recognising that these difficulties are most probably not due to our shortcomings or those of children we teach is very worthwhile in the face of increased concerns about teacher welfare (DfE, 2010; Gibbs, 2007) and also in the realistic appraisal of our influence. With some individuals and on some issues, our behaviours and skills are unlikely to have a substantial impact on their own – a very good reason for involving other professional in our setting, or wider professionals such as school counsellors or educational psychologists. This underlines the importance of a whole-team, whole-setting approach to the welfare of children with dyslexia and other forms of SEND.

A robust research-informed basis for educational interventions and wider practice by educators seeks to minimise the likely psychological harm done to children who have dyslexia or other forms of SEND on account of their difficulties. For example, many accounts in research encourage educators to consider a long-term ('lifespan') perspective on the learning and development of children with dyslexia, in contrast to a shorter-term focus on attainment and qualifications. Critical questioning of everyday educational practice can lead to highly valuable pragmatic questions about the nature of support currently offered to a child. For example:

- Are the short-term, medium-term and long-term academic and personal targets set for this child actually realistic? How do we know (what data do we have)?
- What personal and academic goals does the child have? Do we know? Do these match the formal targets set?
- Is the manner of support contributing to a child's sense of 'difference'? Have we considered this?
- Is the child's (social and emotional) wellbeing considered by those directly involved in their education and care? To what extent?

Relationships in context

JOE (aged 16): I didn't care at school – I used to upset the teachers: shouting, swearing, laughing at them. I stopped going to school before they excluded me.

INTERVIEWER: You don't do that now. What has changed?

JOE: [laughs] No, it's not cool. I want to be at college. I want to do well.

To understand the connections between dyslexia and behaviour further, we need to consider these issues more deeply and beyond what we obviously see in a child/young person's actions or words. Consider Joe above. This was a young man, aged 16, with dyslexia whom I interviewed while conducting research into how young people with dyslexia considered themselves psychologically and in reaction to the label of dyslexia (Armstrong and Humphrey, 2009). Joe was struggling academically but his tutors at that time reported no issues with his behaviour and described him in class as 'diligent and quiet'. In contrast, Joe had a problematic educational history: he had stopped attending school; had been involved with 'gangs'; had poor behaviour when he was attending school; and had been excluded, aged 13.

What is important in the above exchange is how Joe compares two versions of himself. The unsuccessful self (attending high school) and the successful learner (attending college). Joe's self, at 16, is one where college is 'cool' and valuable. Although he is struggling academically, he is motivated 'to do well'. Significantly, none of the previous (aged 13) behaviours (shouting, swearing and laughing) are mentioned: the 'Joe, aged 16' has different (more positive) behaviours in keeping with his different, less troubled self. This suggests that specific changes in his behaviour are connected with specific change in Joe's sense of who he is in an educational setting. This commonplace example has wider, important connections with psychological theory and educational practice. Joe, in this sense, is representative of the issues we often find in the connections between dyslexia and behaviour.

The 'development self' of learners

A deepening interest in children/young people's 'developing self' crystallised in the late 1980s and 1990s around the notion that low/poor self-esteem among children might act as a barrier to academic success and was implicated in more specific (and very diverse) negatives: poor academic motivation; drug and alcohol use; educational disaffection; poor behaviours in the classroom; and low expectations of education (Humphrey, 2004). Covington (2000) sees self-esteem as having an important role in educational policy. Studies have shown working on self-esteem through counselling to be more effective in improving reading skills than spending the same time on remedial teaching (Lawrence, 1985). Attention to the wider psychological welfare of a child has had an increasingly pervasive influence on the work of teachers, psychologists, educationalists and policy-makers (DCSF, 2009a; DfES, 2004, 2005b, 2007; Mowat, 2009; Steer, 2009). Recent manifestations of this trend, in the UK and elsewhere, have centred around enhancing the emotional literacy of children.

Such initiatives have not, however, been without critics. These have questioned the educational efficacy of improving how children/young people feel about themselves (Baumeister *et al.*, 2003) or have claimed that the 'self-esteem movement' is in decline (Dweck, 2002). A key argument has been to question whether improved self-esteem has any relationship with improved academic study or academic achievements (Baumeister *et al.*, 2003). Other authors have pointed out that a child's experience of failure can lead to them reducing their attempts to learn. There is a degree of emotional blocking and a self-view that they may not be successful at learning, saying, 'What is the point in trying?' (Squires and McKeown, 2003 , 2006). A vicious circle is created in which failure leads to further erosion of self-belief and self-esteem and this, in turn, leads to more resistance to learning, which itself leads to further disparity between the child and his or her peers. It is the opposite effect for successful learners, in whom positive experiences lead to more attempts to learn – an effect that has been termed the 'Matthew effect' (Stanovich, 1986). Whatever the truth in these debates for children with dyslexia, it appears that their sense of self (positive, negative or mixed) is often a critical factor in their chances of educational success and the kinds of interventions/support which may or may not be successful to enable this.

The self-system: a concise summary

Returning to Joe, to whom I referred earlier, we might suggest that his academic 'self-esteem' had, in some sense, improved at the age of 16, when compared to his earlier, more troubled self, aged 13. Certainly, his current teachers and tutors did not refer to him as having low/poor self-esteem.

Joe's teachers, like many others across the UK, Australia, the US and elsewhere did, however, often refer to self-esteem in relation to other children with dyslexia, ADHD and other forms of SEND. Self-esteem is not a clear concept and it seems to mean widely different things to different individual professionals (Mruk, 1999).

O'Mara *et al.* (2006) suggest that the term 'self-esteem' has many popular or 'folk' uses which are not always applied accurately or understood clearly by those who using them. One view of self-esteem is that it is an evaluation that we make of how we think we are compared to our ideal view of how we would like to be. Self-esteem is high if the gap between how we perceive ourselves to be and our ideal self is small.

Self-esteem can be a problem when:

- An individual sets unrealistically high aspirations for themselves and sees an ideal self that is unobtainable – the ideal self is too high, so self-esteem is low.
- An individual undervalues their own performance and does not recognise their own achievements – the perceived self is too low and way below the ideal self.
- Ideal selfs are created by other people – for example, governments that determine what level of attainment in a restricted set of subjects should be met by all children; pushy parents who want their child to be the best child in the world.
- The individual sets out low expectations that are easily met to protect self-esteem, but then this does not provide a degree of motivation to strive to be better.

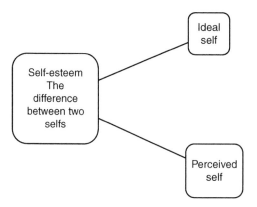

Figure 4.1 Self-esteem as an evaluation.

Some authors have reminded us that there are other factors to consider that influence self-esteem (Armstrong and Humphrey, 2009; Humphrey, 2012; Marsh, 1985):

- Self-esteem is derived from social interaction in the home, school and classroom.
- It is idiosyncratic: an individual's unique life experiences can shape their sense of self in divergent ways.
- It develops in a cumulative way: the attributions of significant others (e.g. parents, peers, teachers) are internalised over time.
- It is multidimensional and hierarchical in nature: an individual can have poor *academic* self-esteem, yet have a positive 'global' sense of self because they excel at sport, art or other areas of endeavour considered valuable by peers, teachers, parents, wider society.

In any society in which literacy is highly prized, such as in Australia, the UK and the US, and in education systems which are increasingly predicated upon school/child performance, we might predict that children who struggle with literacy (among other aspects of study) are likely to face threats to their self-system. This prediction has been explored, and to some extent supported, by research into the experiences of students with dyslexia.

Increased attention to the negative educational and social experiences for children with dyslexia

Running historically alongside these debates about self-esteem and the self-system has been a small but increasing body of accounts which have chronicled and explored the often appalling educational experiences of children with specific learning difficulties. These have been likened to psychological scars (Edwards, 1994) or described as a kind of living nightmare (Osmond, 1993). A commonality among dyslexic children interviewed for research has been a collapse in academic confidence and signs of general psychological distress (Riddick, 1996). Riddick's research consistently underscored how children with dyslexia faced considerable life stresses on account of their educational difficulties. This central finding might also be seen as prefiguring recent interest within educational psychology in fostering positive psychological practices among children in order to enable them to deal with difficult or stressful life experiences (Noble and McGrath, 2008).

An identified weakness within some of this first phase of research was the extent to which it dwelt upon the negative psychological, emotional and social consequences of having dyslexia (Humphrey and Mullins, 2002).

Much of the evidence presented was anecdotal rather than systematic in its enquiry (Burden and Burdett, 2007). This first phase of research, arguably, anchored the foundations for an (ongoing) second round of more focused enquiry into possible relationships between self-system, dyslexia and a child's outcomes, academic and otherwise (Armstrong and Humphrey, 2009). An important outcome of this increased focus was the suggestion of a significantly increased chance of mental health needs among adults with dyslexia (Alexander-Passe, 2012). If correct, then this has major implications for educational practice and policy around mental health services for students in late childhood and adolescence, particularly since many of those dyslexic adults affected reported that their deterioration in mental health began in middle to late adolescence (Alexander-Passe, 2012). This suggestion has added significance when dyslexia is considered in the context of EBD/SEBD and other labels involving behaviour and applied to children in the education systems in the English-speaking world.

SEBD/EBD: enigmatic constructs

There is a lack of agreed international definition as to what constitutes the category of emotional and behavioural difficulties (Hallam and Rogers, 2008). In the UK, SEBD is an important but problematic umbrella construct which has fallen under the Special Educational Needs policy (DFES, 2001). Children described as having SEBD were addressed in flurry of legislation and initiatives/guidance on educational practice from 1980 onwards (DfES, 2004, 2005b, 2007; Goodman and Burton, 2010; HMSO, 1989; OFSTED, 2005; Steer, 2009). There has been some symmetry in the definition of SEBD within UK policy and that in other countries: particularly the US (Harden et al., 2003) and some mainland European countries such as the Netherlands, where there is a significant difference of emphasis – with a medical discourse prevalent (Mooij and Smeets, 2009). More recently, the emphasis has shifted in the UK with the dropping of the word behaviour while retaining a focus on social and emotional wellbeing (DfE and DoH, 2013a). SEBD in the UK has overlapped significantly with other major issues of concern to successive governments, the teaching profession and parents (Hart, 2010). These include mental health needs in children/ young people; poor behaviour and 'discipline' in UK educational settings; the professional role and remit of educators, often expressed by the comment that 'teachers are not social workers'. To some extent, these same professional concerns about behaviour and attitudes towards student behaviours are also present internationally among educators (Hallett and Armstrong, 2012). In the UK, the recent white paper (DfE, 2010) and its emphasis upon the importance of 'good behaviour' is the latest iteration of these concerns. In the US there appear to be similar social dynamics/historical conditions at play (Soles *et al.*, 2008). In this way, concerns about children with SEBD can be seen in the context of wider social concerns about behaviour, which we highlighted at the start of this chapter.

A useful but, not entirely perfect, way to consider SEBD, in these confused circumstances, is to think of it as referring to major barriers for a child's everyday emotional and/or social functioning, with impacts on their ability to form or sustain relationships (DfE, 2001). What an educator might describe as 'poor' behaviour is a likely, although not certain, outcome of these difficulties. Formally, SEBD is defined as a 'high-incidence' difficulty, alongside dyslexia, and, indeed, there appear to be strong, although contested, associations between SEBD and other high-incidence forms of SEND such as dyslexia (Frederickson and Cline, 2009). In this sense, Joe's educational history would seem to be typical of many young people. In fact, it is highly likely that Joe's formal assessment, had it taken place, would have assessed to what extent he might have SEBD alongside the substantive difficulties associated with dyslexia.

Identifying SEBD

If we can't agree on what constitutes SEBD, then it becomes increasingly difficult to decide how assessment should be undertaken (Frederickson and Cline, 2009). Factors that enhance this challenge include the sheer conceptual elasticity of SEBD and also, potentially, professional, political and institutional pressures from educators because of the problematic behaviours shown by children and young people which underpin referral (Mowat, 2009). In the UK, this difficulty in assessing behavioural difficulties within educational contexts was one of the driving forces for the development of the profession of educational psychology at the turn of the twentieth century (Squires, 2012). Educational psychologists and school psychologists in many countries continue to have a major role in orchestrating assessment around SEBD.

For practitioners, knowing when and how to support affected children can be a major dilemma. This is particularly the case where challenging behaviours are being presented alongside the often substantial study difficulties associated with dyslexia. In such cases the two factors can have a synergistic, mutually reinforcing effect, making a meaningful response to the situation very difficult. There is the added challenge that a child's primary difficulties may be behavioural; this leads to a lack of engagement with learning and limited progress in literacy, so the child then appears to be dyslexic.

Connections

Reconsidering research around a child's developing self offers insights in the context of the challenges faced by children with dyslexia. Additionally, a diagnosis of dyslexia might globally and locally affect the child's sense of self (Armstrong and Humphrey, 2009; Burden, 2005; Humphrey, 2012). The exact nature of these changes, whether positive or negative, depends upon a complex set of factors: attitudes of significant others such as teachers; availability of a supportive peer group; how the 'diagnosis' is framed (see Chapter 3), availability of assistive technologies to overcome educational difficulties; availability of special talents by individuals to overcome any academic difficulties. The overlap between SEBD (and other forms of SEND) can be a complicating factor here in terms of whether a label around behaviour can, in some way, contribute to the issues it describes around a child. This also relates to the whole issue of labelling practice for dyslexia: an important issue for practice discussed in the preceding chapter.

It is, however, highly significant that many, if not most, of these factors are not, in any way, attributable solely to the behaviour of the child affected. Behaviour here is the reaction (positive, ambivalent or negative) we see to the situation in which the child finds him/herself and in relation to the challenges often faced by children with dyslexia in educational settings. For practitioners, this view avoids the pejorative and unhelpful connotations inherent in a 'within child' view of children with disability. It also offers the potential for a structured and meaningful analysis of behaviour such as that proposed, for example, by functional behaviour analysis and other systematic ways of gathering information about behaviour in order to come to a reasoned view about how to respond.

A further key part of this deeper conceptualisation of behaviour is considering our own behaviours and that of colleagues. This takes the emphasis way from the child and recognises, instead, that teachers, pupils and parents are in (often complex) relationships.

Relationships: recognising our own psychological resources

In our experience many educators underestimate the psychological impact that their daily efforts have on them, in attempting to resolve these tensions arising from an imperfect educational system for children with SEND. This is exacerbated by politically driven targets, performance criteria and initiatives which governments in Australia, the UK, US and elsewhere periodically subject teachers to. It is not surprising if this situation has consequences for the quality of relationships around school (teacher/professionals–pupil–parent). These relationships are the subject of ongoing and important international research within psychology and education (Elik *et al.*, 2010). Some researchers in this area highlight that it is teachers themselves who report that they are effectively disabled by an increasingly performance-driven education system (Hallett and Armstrong, 2012).

Recognising when, and to what extent, our own psychological state interferes with our relationships with others can be part of an important personal strategy for teachers. This knowledge can aid decision-making and performance in potentially stressful situations (Zimmerman and Schunk, 2013).

Functional behavioural analysis (FBA)

In the context of dealing with situations involving what we regard as problematic behaviours by children or young people with dyslexia, the point made at the end of the section above is extremely relevant. In particular situations, the best strategy might be to stand back, cease our behaviours and try to observe *exactly* what is happening, taking note of time and context. This exact, structured analysis of behaviour is a key element in FBA, an important concept which has received support from research as a potentially effective behaviour strategy for educators to use (Armstrong, 2013; Cooper, 2011).

In the US, FBA has been identified as an evidence-based approach under legislation and designated for use with children who are at risk of educational exclusion on account of their behaviour (US Department of Education, 2004). The use of FBA includes a very structured data-gathering process, leading to production of a data-driven behavioural intervention plan which sets out how that student's needs can be met (New Mexico Education Department, 2010). It is important to stress here that FBA is additional and separate to the usual repertoire of techniques used by most educators in response to behaviours they encounter, such as 'low-level' disruption (Hallam and Rogers, 2008).

FBA has significant shared territory with applied behaviour analysis (Lovitt, 2012). Its origin lies in Skinner's work on behaviourism; the underlying principle is that behaviour improves when it is rewarded. Having a basis in applied behaviour analysis, the use of functional analysis declined over the 1980s, but has recently started to undergo a resurgence (Cone, 1997). Functional analysis techniques have been described as having 'significantly influenced the understanding and treatment of challenging behaviour' (O'Reilly, 1996) and as one of the most common and successful tools used for analysing challenging behaviour to improve treatment effectiveness (Healey *et al.*, 2001; Matson *et al.*, 1999; Roane *et al.*, 1999; Tincani *et al.*, 1999). It has been described as the 'most potent and effective behavioural assessment methodology for disorders associated with developmental disabilities' (Vollmer and Smith, 1996). This makes functional analysis a clinical pre-intervention assessment tool worthy of further consideration. FBA has moved on a little and requires the person who is trying to understand the behaviour to take the perspective of the person displaying the behaviour. It starts with the simple idea that all behaviours serve a function for the individuals who present them. The observer can think about the behaviour as a message that is communicating something about what the other person wants. In this sense, all behaviours are rational to the person who is carrying them out. They are only maladaptive or challenging if they cause problems in the context in which the behaviour is being exhibited. There may be more adaptive responses that can be taught by the teacher. The task of FBA is to work out what is the communicative function of the behaviour.

When we engage in functional analysis we are looking at some aspect of behaviour and we are trying to give it some meaning for the person displaying the behaviour. We are attempting to attribute some reason for the behaviour and are treating it as being purposeful and not a random act. This is different from purer behavioural approaches that look at antecedents and stimuli leading to the behaviour and reinforcement schedules that maintain the behaviour. These are still important in functional analysis, but an extra dimension is added through the consideration of the other person's perspective and the attributing of intentionality and meaningfulness of the behaviour. Functional analysis also differs from more traditional behavioural approaches that rely on differential reinforcement by considering the ways in which the environment can be modified (Norgate, 1998).

Functional analysis requires consideration of:

- The actual behaviours exhibited, when these occur and how often.
- The ecology in which the behaviour occurs – the antecedents leading to the behaviour in terms of physical setting, social circumstances, specific stimuli, task demands.
- Reinforcement schedules to increase, decrease or maintain the behaviour, and whether these are intended or occur as a result of the organisational or social conditions.
- The potential communicative intent of the behaviour from the perspective of the person displaying the behaviour.
- Whether the behaviour is correlated to any of these factors or whether there is a causal link. In functional analysis we are interested in finding causal explanations for behaviour. Why is the person presenting with challenging behaviour?

Some basic motivational categories can be used to assist this process, such as considering whether the behaviour presented fits into one or more of the following categories (and if so why and what can be done to address this):

- to obtain tangibles;
- attention;
- power/control;
- escape/avoidance;
- revenge;
- anxiety avoidance or reduction.

FBA offers a structured strategy for educators to use with children who have significant behavioural issues of the kind sometimes presented alongside dyslexia. For example, if a child is presented with some work by the teacher, then presents a serious challenge to the flow of the lesson by throwing a tantrum, we can start by considering what the tantrum means. The tantrum only occurs in the classroom setting when the work is presented. The work involves writing. The child is dyslexic and finds writing hard. The tantrum could signify anger at the teacher for giving work that cannot be done. Or it could be an escape strategy to avoid having to do the work. Previous experience has taught the child that when she throws a tantrum she gets sent out of the room to the principal's office and misses the work being done. Moreno and Bullock (2011) explain this type of behaviour in terms of antecedents (work given), behaviours (tantrum) and consequences (does not have to do the work). In their description, they maintain the position of observers. It is more effective in FBA to take the position of the pupil and to think about what the behaviour is saying.

Functional analysis can be broken down to distinct phases:

- **Descriptive phase**: deciding and agreeing on what the behaviour is that generates concern among staff. This involves systematic data collection.
- **Interpretative phase**: using the information to inform hypotheses about why the behaviour is occurring. What is the meaning or purpose of the behaviour from the perspective of the person displaying the behaviour? This is essentially about generating hunches or ideas about what might be going on and why.
- **Evaluative phase or verification phase**: this involves the experimental testing out of the different hypotheses generated to establish the most likely explanation. The correct identification of the cause of the behaviour then allows consideration of interventions aimed at reducing challenging behaviour while maximising the quality of life for the person.

Often, the first two parts of this process are done and the evaluation is missed. This is referred to as functional *assessment* rather than functional *analysis* (Cone, 1997; Vollmer and Smith, 1996).

The first phase is to describe the behaviour accurately. The purpose of this phase is to gather information about: the precise nature of the behaviour; the potentially relevant contextual variables; the events immediately prior to the behaviour (antecedents); and the events immediately after the behaviour (consequents).

These are the kinds of questions that might be useful:

- In as much detail as possible, describe what the individual actually does.
- When does the behaviour seem to occur more or less?
- Who is present or absent?
- Who is working with the individual?
- Where does this behaviour seem to occur?
- Are there particular objects or materials that seem to make the behaviour worse (or better)?
- What happens if a particular object, food or toy is removed?
- What tasks are being undertaken?
- What was happening before the behaviour occurred?
- Did anything happen before the session?
- What happens at the time of the behaviour?
- What happens after the behaviour has occurred?

The second step is one of interpretation in order to come up with possible explanations of why the behaviour is occurring. These are likely to be 'best guesses' or 'hunches' and should be treated as tentative hypotheses.

This process can be informal or can involve a number of prearranged steps to organise the information collected into possible causality relationships. Cone (1997) describes several approaches which are commonly used:

- During the descriptive phase the observer records frequency of behaviour and starts to add perceived functions. During the interpretive phase the functions are examined to establish patterns and formulate hypotheses about controlling relationships.
- During the descriptive phase the behaviours are written on separate cards as they occur. On each card the observer also writes the antecedent and consequent social events. During the interpretative phase, the cards are grouped according to the hypothesised function. The interpretation is carried out by three people – two who were involved in completing the cards and a third person not involved. Each person reads the cards independently and asks himself or herself, 'What do

you think the person wanted to happen as a result of performing this behaviour?' The panel then discuss their interpretations and only keep the cards that two out of three (or all of them) could agree on.

The third phase is to evaluate the hunches. Having come up with different possible explanations, this part of the process is concerned with testing out whether one of the explanations is better than the others, or, indeed, whether any of the explanations are good enough. This might be through formal manipulation of the circumstances surrounding the behaviour or might be an informal test. For example, if the hypothesis is that Jane squeals loudly when she is waiting so that she can engage adult attention, then we might decide 'to see what happens if we ignore her'.

Experimental manipulation of problematic behaviour to validate or question different hypotheses involves devising a functional analysis probe. This is a scenario in which different aspects of the hypothesis can be manipulated. This raises a number of concerns:

- It is time consuming. However, once one hypothesis has been verified above others, the time spent can be recouped or saved by devising a more efficient intervention. We are concerned with trying to design an intervention that removes the underlying cause of the problematic behaviour.
- It may involve allowing people to engage in dangerous behaviours (e.g. self-injurious behaviour, running out of school). This can be dealt with by setting a maximum number of occurrences of the target behaviour before intervention or terminating the probe. Protective clothing or helmets could be used, adults could be strategically placed at exits. Alternatively, the time between the stimuli and the behaviour occurring could be timed (latency) so that the dangerous behaviour is prevented through intervention. Latency could be used to measure the different conditions being manipulated.

The questions needed in deciding what to do in this phase depend upon the hypotheses formulated, but are essentially about:

- what to manipulate (setting, events and tasks, antecedents, consequents);
- how to manipulate it;
- what criteria to use to decide whether control has been achieved. (Are there contextual supports for the problem behaviour? In other words, what combination leads to a lessening of the problem behaviour?)

Figure 4.2 summarises the main stages in the functional analysis process. Functional analysis leads into intervention planning.

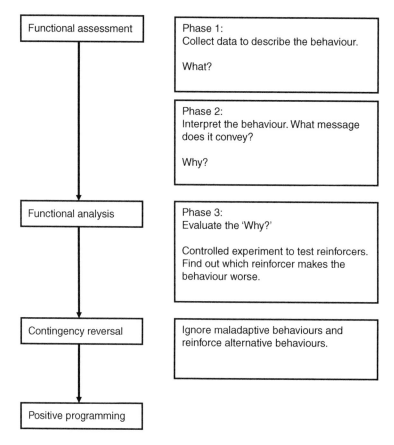

Figure 4.2 Steps in FBA.

Hanbury (2012), who is a highly experienced practitioner, also makes an insightful comment about the dilemma which can occur for educators in terms of selecting priorities for addressing a student's behaviour. He proposes that we carefully consider our priorities for practice with each case, mindful that we have choices which will vary between children and cases, but which offer the following basic options:

- Focus entirely on the need with the most profound influence.
- Address a hierarchy of needs and select those that are the most influential first.
- Focus attention on an area of need in proportion to its influence on the child or the classroom.

Other emotional difficulties related to dyslexia

Most education systems value reading and writing, and there is an emphasis on success in these areas as children progress through mass education systems. This can be problematic for those children who fail to acquire literacy skills as quickly as their peers and can lead to unhelpful emotional responses and mental health difficulties. The experiences that children receive, the way they are presented to children and the messages that go alongside those experiences can all have negative effects on emotional wellbeing. This can be exacerbated by anxious parents and teachers who transfer their worries onto the child or use labels that lead to a deterioration of self-esteem:

- 'You're useless at spelling!'
- 'You're in the bottom group.'
- 'You need special help for reading.'
- 'Everyone else can read … why can't you? You're lazy!'
- 'No, that book is too hard for you … have this one.'

The emotional response of the child will become more significant with age (Charlton, 1992). The experience of failure to read leads to demotivation or emotional blocking. This, in turn, leads to the child avoiding reading and reduces the expenditure of effort and persistence in trying to read. This then leads to a reduction in reading experience and less success compared to peers. The child sees the gap between themselves and their peers appear to get wider and this increases their emotional response, further eroding self-esteem and belief in themselves as an independent learner.

The cycle continues, leading to what Stanovich (1986) calls the 'Matthew effect': good readers get comparatively better while poor readers get comparatively worse. The difference between a good reader and a poor reader becomes more obvious to teachers and to the children themselves. This means that the emotional impact of dyslexia cannot be ignored; in some studies, working on self-esteem through counselling has been shown to be more effective in improving reading skills than spending the same time on remedial teaching (Lawrence, 1985). In this chapter we are going to explore some of the difficulties and the processes at play.

Learned helplessness

It may seem odd that in our education systems we can inadvertently teach children not to learn. This is an accidental consequence of the way that we organise education. In an ideal world, there would be one teacher for every pupil who could then perfectly match teaching to learning and present material in a way that provided just enough support for the child to succeed. Too much support would mean that the child would not be challenged and their learning stretched and too little support would mean that the tasks would be too hard and the child would not learn because they could not succeed. In a mass education system, the class teacher has to endeavour to create this ideal learning state with many pupils, who will have different learning needs. It is a tall order and one that is hard to achieve. The logical next best approach would seem to be to provide more adult support to those pupils who are making less progress. This approach has been widely adopted through the provision of teaching assistants, who work in the classroom alongside the teacher and with pupils who need additional support to learn. In England, the number of teaching assistants used in schools rose rapidly from 64,200 in 1997 to 103,600 in 2002 and to 181, 600 in 2009 (DCSF, 2009b; DfES, 2002).

To be used effectively, there needs to be good co-ordination and leadership from the class teacher so that supported pupils can be part of the main class and engage in a full range of activities while having more intensive teaching for part of the lesson. Logically, we would expect children who have teaching assistants working with them to make more progress than children who do not. However, this may not be the case. Schools lack capacity and budgets are tight, meaning that adults are often fully employed in face to face contact with pupils. Teachers do not have time set aside to allow them to co-ordinate, plan jointly, or share monitoring information with teaching assistants, and teaching assistants may be poorly trained (Blatchford *et al.*, 2009a, 2009b; Cajkler *et al.*, 2007). A more recent study suggests that the more support children get, the less academic progress they make (Webster *et al.*, 2010). These studies tell us about general patterns emerging from the support that pupils receive; there are some very good working relationships between teachers and teaching assistants and some very skilled teaching assistants that can work well with children.

One of the negative effects of too much adult support is that the child develops a degree of learned helplessness. They appear to give up, over-rely on adult support and will not independently attempt tasks that are well within their capability. When pupils stop trying with learning tasks, this reduces their ability to learn and problem solve. Over time, they become more and more dependent on adult support and less and less willing to attempt literacy tasks. Learned helplessness is a learned dependency and is often associated with faulty beliefs such as, 'I must not be able to do it otherwise Miss would not be helping me. After all, she doesn't help anyone else!'

The way in which support is organised within the classroom and around the learning task can help to reduce the development of learned helplessness.

We want to achieve the same outcome for the dyslexic reader as we do for the non-dyslexic reader – namely, independent learning and a perception from the child that they are a successful learner. Here are a few questions that can be asked to help achieve this goal:

- Can I support a small group of children rather than an individual?
- Can I ask questions that provide prompts to encourage the child to think about strategies to use in order to solve the problem for themselves?
- How can I direct the child's attention to the important features of words when reading?
- How can I encourage the child to make comparisons with words that they already know?
- Can I encourage the child to take risks with learning – for example, by guessing, praising their attempts, showing them where they have been successful (even if only partially)?
- I am emotionally strong enough to refuse to help a child when I know that the task is well within their capability? Good monitoring of children's performance should mean that adults can remind the child of other occasions when they were able to do this task.
- How can I fade support as the child becomes more competent so that I am only providing the minimum level of help and encouraging the child to be independent? Can I leave the child longer before providing input, while at the same time expressing an expectation that they will successfully complete at least part of the task unaided?
- Can I make use of flow charts to take the child through routine procedures to increase the amount of time spent working independently from the teacher?
- Can I make use of forward chaining? This where the child starts off the first few steps of the problem and the adult helps them complete it. Gradually increasing the number of steps that the child is asked to do moves them towards greater independence.
- Can I make use of backwards chaining? In this case, the adult starts off the problem solving, leaving the child to complete the last few steps. As with forwards chaining, gradually increasing the number of steps that the child is asked to do moves them towards greater independence.

Comparison with peers

Most of the time, we like to think of ourselves as being similar to those around us. We describe ourselves as 'normal' and we tend to like to be like everyone else (despite our claims of individuality). Similarly, children do not like to be seen as being widely different from their peers. This is a problem which seems to become more acute as they reach adolescence. This has several major effects in school:

- The child compares themselves to peers in terms of performance and particularly poor performance with literacy.
- The child does not want to be singled out in class by having a 'helper' sit with them.
- The child engages in other ego-protective behaviours that are not acceptable to the school, such as wanting to be popular with peers and becoming the 'class clown' or actively rejecting literacy-based activities and becoming challenging to the teacher.

In the first case, the child's self-esteem can be protected by having a positive class ethos in which each child is valued for what they can do. The teacher is able to show the child in a positive light in classroom activities and allow the child to demonstrate competence in some activities in front of their peers. The teacher tries hard to avoid depreciating remarks that carry the messages 'You are useless/worthless and a waste of space.'

Parents have a role to play in this as well. It is easy for parents' anxieties and worries about a lack of progress to be contained in unintentional messages to the child. This might be because the child sees the parent always at school talking to the teacher and having 'worried conversations'. In some schools this is mitigated by having an open atmosphere where parents regularly meet with teachers at the end of the day. In this case, the children could be given a task to do while the parent and teacher talk. Another strategy is to have a home–school book in which positive comments and concerns are exchanged.

In England, the Code of Practice for Special Educational Needs (0–25) places an emphasis on children being involved in their assessment and having a voice in person-centred reviews. This is best managed by having the child present as an equal partner in review meetings and having a discussion with a positive framing. This means that positive messages are used that focuses on success – what can the child do today that they could not do yesterday? This can lead to current concerns, shared goals for progress and actions to be taken next.

Performance anxiety

One of the effects of continuing to fail in an environment that expects high levels of performance is that it leads to anxiety whenever the person has to perform publically; this becomes generalised beyond the initial experiences that led to it. In school, pupils become reluctant to try in front of their classmates (social anxiety); they may become anxious around examinations (test anxiety); or they may complete course work tasks but avoid giving them in. These types of problems can continue beyond school and into work or university.

A cognitive model for thinking about emotional responses

Cognitive behavioural therapy has been successfully applied with adults to help with a range of emotional difficulties; it was originally developed for dealing with anxiety and depression (Beck and Emery, 1979; Beck *et al.*, 1985; Beck et al., 1990; Beck *et al.*, 1979; Emery, 1985). Central to this model is the idea that thoughts, feelings and behaviours are linked. Our emotional responses depend upon our interpretation of what is going on around us and this helps us to decide what we will do in that situation. How we interpret the situation depends upon our past experiences. With repeated experiences of similar situations, our thinking becomes habitual and automatic. Most of the time this is a good thing – the world that we inhabit is generally safe and we are generally competent.

Supposing that our experiences around literacy have always been that reading and writing were difficult things to do; that the task is a threatening task because we might fail; that other children seem to be smarter than us because they find reading easy. Then what might we think about ourselves and how might this affect our willingness to engage in learning? We might see ourselves as 'thick' or 'stupid' or not successful as a learner. This might lead to us feeling resentment when we are asked to undertake a reading task, to feeling bad about ourselves, to feeling anxious. A whole range of possibilities exist.

In time, we start to anticipate these thoughts and feelings and this leads to us becoming anxious before the task is presented. We start to interpret stimuli, which might otherwise be benign, as threatening. For example, Jane is asked to read out in class. An automatic thought flashes through her head so quickly that she is unaware of it: 'I'm useless at reading.' She thinks, 'I'll probably make mistakes and the other kids will laugh.' She becomes motivated to avoid the situation: 'If I get sent out I won't have to do this.' Emotional responses might include feeling ashamed or even angry that the teacher is putting her through this ordeal. She may even think that the teacher hates her – why else would she make her feel like this? Further evaluations of the situation might lead her to notice David smiling. Another automatic thought enters play: 'He's laughing at me.' This leads to the behaviour – verbal or physical abuse of the child who smiled. This is the behaviour the teacher sees and Jane is sent out of the room.

The child can be supported by helping them become aware of automatic thoughts. The relevance of the automatic thought to the current situation can then be checked out and alternatives offered. What else could David have been smiling at? Perhaps he was laughing at you. Perhaps he was pleased to see you were chosen. Maybe, he was smiling at the girl behind you. Perhaps he was pleased because the teacher had just said how pleased she was with his reading. The child is taught to ask a series of questions to check out their response:

- How do we know which possibility is true?
- How can you find out? What evidence can you get?
- How would you feel in each case?
- How strongly?
- What would you do in each case?

Life experiences can contribute to the development of core beliefs about self. When these lead to difficulties they tend to be beliefs such as:

- beliefs about the world (e.g. the world is a dangerous place);
- beliefs about other people (e.g. other people are better than me, smarter than me);
- beliefs about self (e.g. I am not worthy, I am useless).

The core beliefs lead to a set of rules or assumptions that Melanie Fennell refers to as 'rules for living' (Fennell, 1999).

Case example

Robert is a Year 8 pupil at a middle school. His teachers say that he is well behaved and reasonably clever, but that he never completes any work that is set. The background information collected from teachers told me that Robert's mother had died when he was aged two years old. His dad worked as a long-distance lorry driver and was often away from home. Robert and his older brother had to look after themselves when their dad was away. There had been other partners – but most only stayed for a few months. Social services had been involved in the past. Sometimes, the dad took the boys with him on one of his trips (but this meant that they missed school).

When I first worked with Robert, I wanted to establish some baseline measures on how he saw himself. I asked him to complete the Beck Youth Inventory and stressed that I only wanted him to do the first 20 items. The items were well within Robert's reading ability range and he started to do the task quietly by himself, while I marked some other assessments that he had completed. Each item requires the pupil to draw a circle around one

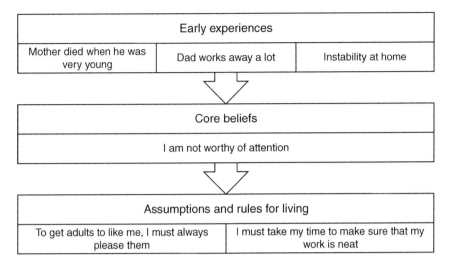

Figure 4.3 Rules for living.

of four words to rate the degree it applies to them or not. As I watched Robert, he moved his hand slowly around each word to make a perfect and very neat circle. Each answer took between 30 and 40 seconds to draw. Once he reached the end of the page and completed the first 20 items, he turned the page and worked through the next set of items in the same way. Robert went on to complete all five pages (taking an hour to do so). I was able to discuss this with him afterwards with one question in mind, 'What might have been going on for him?'

The trigger for Robert was being asked to do any writing. He would always laboriously take his time. Every letter had to be perfectly printed. He worried that he would make a mistake and that, if he did, then teachers would use red ink on his page and they would give him bad marks. He said that if his dad heard about this then he would not be pleased. He thought that his dad would 'get in a grump' and would not talk to him.

There was a feedback loop for Robert. As a consequence of him not completing his work, his teachers had contacted his father and asked him to come into school. His dad had been upset. This confirmed one of Robert's predictions – his dad was displeased, sulked and did not speak to him. In Robert's eyes, this confirmed his core belief – he was not worthy of attention. Self-critical thoughts followed, 'I'm stupid'; 'I can't do any work good enough to please my teachers or my dad.' This, in turn, contributed to low mood, low self-esteem and lack of motivation.

The core belief is open to change if evidence can be presented that disconfirms it. However, without intervention, Robert continues to treat

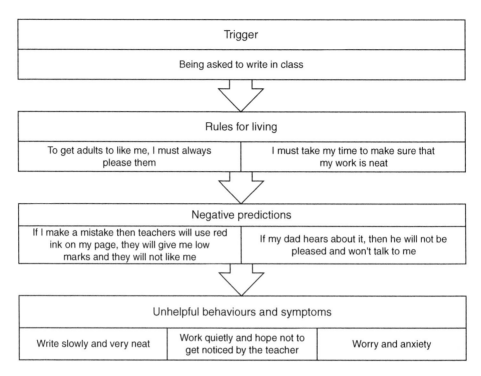

Figure 4.4 Unhelpful behaviours.

the belief as if it is a fact. This means that the next time that Robert is asked to do some writing he will have to try extra hard to make sure that it is neat enough to make his teachers happy. Only then will they like him. If they like him, then they won't call his dad. If his dad doesn't hear any bad news about him in school then he may like him more and take him on one of his trips away.

Improving self-monitoring is a useful approach to take in understanding how these processes work. This allows for different types of intervention, which include:

• Becoming more aware of thoughts, feelings and behaviours and how these relate to each other.
• Considering the evidence for and against particular thoughts, especially those that appear to occur habitually.
• Exploring assumptions and rules for living to identify which are helpful and which were once helpful but are now leading to unhelpful ways of responding. Finding ways to change unhelpful rules for more helpful ones follows.
• Replacing anxious predictions with more helpful predictions and then testing these out through behavioural experiments.

Adults need self-monitoring too: stop for a moment

Consideration of our own self-monitoring can also be helpful in suggesting how we might enhance our relationships with others (pupils, parents and colleagues). Self-monitoring can be 'characterized by an ability to attend, moment to moment, to our own actions; curiosity to examine the effects of those actions; and willingness to use those observations to improve behaviour and patterns of thinking in the future' (Epstein *et al.*, 2008, p. 5).

In essence, self-monitoring is a key part of the feedback loop we use in our interactions with others and in ensuring that these fulfil whatever needs or predispositions we have ('I want the student to attempt to read this sentence'; 'I want this child to succeed in this task here'). Research around improving professional practice, particularly clinical practice, has increasingly emphasised the importance of self-monitoring (Cleary *et al.*, 2012; Leggett *et al.*, 2012). Significantly, psychological stress and physical factors such as lack of sleep can degrade or even entirely prevent self-monitoring: we stop attending to our own actions and the effects of these.

From theory and applied research around the phenomenon of self-regulation we can also glean the idea that self-monitoring is an important factor in terms of the likely success of any complex task or social interaction, particularly effective decision-making (Sniehotta, 2009). If we are not attending carefully to our actions and the reactions of others then we are more likely to make decisions based on false or partial foundations, with unwanted or unpredictable results.

There is, therefore, the potential to develop our self-monitoring; firm research provides evidence that individuals vary significantly in the extent to which they easily develop self-monitoring (Zimmerman and Schunk, 2013). From the above we can deduce, for educators, that:

- If we are tired, suffering from stress or other complications then additional effort might be required in terms of our self-monitoring. Do we ever recognise when our performance is not 'optimum'? When does this happen exactly? Where are we at that moment? What steps do we take to account for this?

We can also, potentially, enhance our self-monitoring by self-prompting. Some initial examples of prompts we might ask ourselves are:

- How am I doing here? Am I fully listening? Am I being listened to?
- Is this working? If not, why not? What do I need to change? If so, why? Can this be developed? Where, exactly?
- What are the reactions to: my suggestions, my directions, my efforts? Positive, ambivalent, negative?
- Do I need to adjust, wholly change or discard my approach, conduct and/or behaviours?

Conclusion

As was outlined at the start of this chapter, behaviour around education settings is often a key issue for children and young people with dyslexia. Indeed, for a significant number of children, issues around behaviour rather than issues around dyslexia per se are the most pressing issue for educators. The sub-group of children who have recognised EBD or SEBD and also co-occurring dyslexia are particularly at risk of a range of negative outcomes and there is some evidence that education systems across the English-speaking world at least have a poor record in supporting their needs (Macleod, 2010). This unsatisfactory state seems to continue despite continued messages from research as to how high the social costs are when children fail educationally through issues around behaviour and/or poor attendance of the kind associated with dyslexia (Hallam and Rogers, 2008).

As was suggested in this chapter, understanding our own role and behaviours can be a key tool in dealing with the varied situations in which we find ourselves in the classroom. To re-summarise, this has been presented as a helpful perspective which:

1 understands how the child's perception of themselves affects behaviour;
2 takes the focus away from the child and considers our role as part of a relationship;
3 potentially assists professionals to have a more informed, less reactive response to the often challenging behaviours they face;
4 considers how to think about behaviour from the perspective of the child;
5 considers the interplay between thoughts, feelings and behaviours;
6 considers the role of early experiences and development of rules for living and habitual ways of thinking;
7 understands that these things are open to change when the right evidence and self-monitoring techniques are applied.

In the context of this chapter, FBA was also outlined as an example of a classroom strategy which has support from research for responding to children's challenging behaviour and as something discrete and additional to the usual repertoire of behavioural techniques used by educators.

One key, final point to draw from this topic is that fidelity is vital to any strategy, approach or intervention used in relation to a child's behaviour, drawn from theory or research. Put another way, any intervention, strategy or approach is only as good as the quality of its application (fidelity) by a committed professional (specialist teacher) who applies it carefully and as intended. For interested policy-makers, this emphasises the vital role of high-quality, adequately funded professional learning around child and adolescent behaviour throughout a specialist educator's working life.

Chapter summary

- An emphasis upon relationships at every level (as opposed to behaviours) is beneficial. This is likely to involve initiative at a whole-setting level.
- Developing positive relationships should be at the core of practice and institutional policy.
- SEBD is an extremely broad umbrella term: at their core, however, forms of SEBD affect a learners' social-emotional functioning and their development.
- Children with forms of dyslexia often also have forms of SEBD and vice versa: this can complicate interventions.
- Prior to assessment for dyslexia, practitioners should check whether the individual has a formally recognised form of SEBD.
- Motivation, self-esteem and other psychological facets of an individual are important, although complex, factors in their learning and development.
- An essential understanding of FBA and facets of psychological theory (such as self-monitoring) can be helpful in a better understanding of relationships and thereby how we might promote better relationships at school/in a setting.
- Any intervention, strategy or approach drawn from research is only as good as the quality of its application (fidelity).

Reflective questions

- Does your setting have a policy on behaviour – if so are you and colleagues familiar with it?
- What structures, staff and resources (including professional learning) are available to support positive relationships?
- Are learners with dyslexia recognised in your setting as being at elevated risk of social or emotional difficulties? What form does this recognition take?
- What happens when a relationship between an educator and a student has a breakdown or is at risk of breakdown? Is there guidance or a protocol about what to do?

- Are the behaviours of adults/staff recognised in your setting alongside those of children or young people?
- Is diagnostic labelling done wisely and cautiously?
- What resources (including people) are available to assist in sustaining positive professional relationships with students in and around the setting?
- Are there external agencies available to assist with developing better relationships between children and adults in your setting?
- Is 'relationship' a more informed and accurate term than 'behaviour' when considering educational practice with children or young people who have a disability or SEN?

Chapter 5

Intellectual disability, dyslexia and intelligence

Introduction: the explicit and implicit influence of notions about intelligence on practice with disabled learners

Assumptions about intelligence have a profound, if often subtle, influence on discussion across the educational field and in relation to children's schooling (Sternberg and Kaufman, 2012). These undercurrents of thought stretch back to the start of modern education systems in Europe and the English-speaking world. The whole notion of intelligence arose as a result of a crisis in education that required western governments to determine which children would need specialist teaching that could not take place in mainstream schools. Early attempts to measure intelligence were based on ideas of natural variability and this led to intelligence as being thought about as something which is normally distributed within the population. Some people have more and some people have less, and if it can be measured then it can be used to predict academic success. The idea is rooted in genetics and the work of Galton, which led to initial unsuccessful attempts to produce a predictive test by Wissler in 1901. James Cattell introduced the term 'mental aptitude' when trying to assess university students in 1809 (Ittenbach *et al.*, 1997; Thorndike, 1997). Refinements followed through the work of Binet and Simon in 1905 to produce a test suitable for purpose. The term 'IQ' or 'intelligence quotient' was introduced in 1912 by Stern. Further developments of tests to measure mental aptitude followed the First World War and an average IQ was defined by Wechsler as being equal to 100. David Wechsler provides us with a useful definition of what intelligence represents by conceptualising it as 'the capacity of the individual to act purposefully, to think rationally, and to deal effectively with his environment' (Wechsler, 2004).

Intelligence tests have continued to develop and have been widely deployed in our education system. One test used to screen high school students is called the Cognitive Abilities Test (CAT) and this has been found to have higher predictive ability of final examination success than either teacher assessments or Standard Assessment Tests (SATs). The correlations are not perfect; the best correlation is between CAT's quantitative reasoning and maths GCSE performance, accounting for around 49 per cent of the variance (Strand, 2006). This less than perfect correlation means that some writers are sceptical about the use of IQ tests in education.

Entire books have been written about intelligence and its importance for education policy or educational practice. What follows is not intended to replicate this, *but* notions of intelligence expressed in the term 'intelligence quotient' (IQ) are highly relevant to the everyday practice of specialist educators and professionals involved with individuals who present with dyslexia. As we point out, intelligence matters (at least politically) – for example, in the assessment of children with dyslexia and in the important question of how children who are categorised as having intellectual disability (ID) figure in relation to the category of dyslexia.

Intelligence and dyslexia

Modern 'scientific' approaches to intelligence, and everything they entail, arguably began when Alfred Binet, a French scientist, was commissioned in the early twentieth century by the French Ministry of Education to develop tests which could identify mentally defective children. This was so that children defined as intellectually deficient could have separate provision from their 'normal' peers (Binet and Simon, 1916). Since then, many of the practices of educators and features of education systems have been – often in subtle, indirect ways – based on ideas about intelligence, often given the shorthand description of 'ability' by those working in education and in special education.

Research over the last 20 years has increasingly emphasised the importance of *teacher attitudes* and *teacher knowledge* for the nature of practice with children – particularly their influence on these factors for practice with children who have forms of disability and in terms of their educational inclusion (Gibbs and Powell, 2012; Humphrey, 2004). In research about the educational outcomes of children with dyslexia, for example, researchers have sought to identify whether and to what extent the attitudes, decisions and actions of educators might influence what happens to children in terms of later life outcomes (Burden, 2005, 2008; Gwernan-Jones and Burden, 2009). There is a potentially important connection here between 'what happens' (or does not happen) in classrooms and in schools with children who are disabled, on the basis of perceptions about an individual's intelligence. For example, a detailed US study into practice around literacy with children who have ID notes very low levels of expectation by adults: 'In practice it appears that many educators assume that children

| Intelligence is irrelevant: | Intelligence is important: |
| 'Dyslexia is not related to intelligence' | 'Dyslexia is a specific learning difficulty' |

Figure 5.1 Intelligence and dyslexia.

with ID are unlikely to learn to read by fully processing print; rather, efforts have focused on teaching students to memorize specific lists of words' (Allor *et al.*, 2010a; Allor *et al.*, 2010b).

Other, important research about children with dyslexia and also other types of disability, has suggested how awareness of learner's label can also have a dampening *general* effect on teacher expectations of affected children, even in terms of areas of a child's functioning which are unaffected (Hornstra *et al.*, 2010). There is, however, recognition in the research literature that this is a complex area which varies from educator to educator, setting to setting and is also affected by the larger macroclimate around education, including perceived attitudes towards inclusion (Gibbs, 2007).

As was discussed earlier, intelligence tests continue to be used to help decide whether a child has dyslexia or whether difficulties with literacy are more general, which is a subject not without contention. IQ tests were used in reference to the highly influential discrepancy model, where a gap or 'discrepancy' between a student's test score on measures of intelligence was compared with their score on standardised tests of reading, writing and spelling; a significant difference between the two was said to be potentially indicative of dyslexia, particularly in children achieving within the 'normal' or 'above normal' distribution ranges (BPS, 1999; Fletcher, 2012).

There is a folk law around the link between intelligence and dyslexia. This is sometimes explicitly expressed in statements by educators, parents and other stakeholders about affected children in relation to intelligence. These comments are often made, in our experience, on a spectrum illustrated in Figure 5.1.

To make matters more complex – and potentially tricky for a specialist educator practising in this area – garbled and sometimes ill-informed comments about intelligence, disability or dyslexia appear in the electronic and/or print media across the English-speaking world from time to time. Sometimes these can provoke positive policy initiatives around dyslexia (Rose, 2009); at other times these can, arguably, be unhelpful for informed debate and improvement in outcomes for affected children (Elliott and Gibbs, 2008).

Views of disability and dyslexia

As was suggested in the introduction to this book, we propose an operational and pragmatic rather than strictly categorical approach to the definition of dyslexia. This is in line with internationally accepted notions of disability based on a social model of disability and considering an individual's level of functioning in everyday life when thinking about their needs (Riddick, 2001). Under this framework, disability exists as it is socially and functionally experienced by the child or young person and is recognised as affecting them every day in one or more domains of their life. This definition of disability, therefore, bypasses the idea that dyslexia is bound up with a child's 'innate' intelligence and instead focuses on identifying an individual's potential.

In this context, Martha Nussbaum, an influential philosopher based in the US, has suggested a potentially helpful set of ten central capabilities which might act as a wider frame against which to consider educational practice and our impact as educators on learners' development:

1 Life: not dying prematurely or living a life not worth living.
2 Bodily health: having good health (including reproductive health), shelter and food.
3 Bodily integrity: freedom to move around, to be secure from any violence or abuse and to have the opportunity to gain sexual pleasure and have reproductive choices.
4 Senses, imagination and thought: being able to use the senses, think and reason.
5 Emotions: to be able to love, care, grieve and to experience longing, gratitude and justified anger. Not have these thwarted for fear of anxiety.
6 Practical reason: being able to think about the good and reflect about one's life.
7 Affiliation:

   a. Live with and towards others and engage in social interaction.
   b. Have the social bases for self-respect and make provisions for non-discrimination.

8 Other species: concern for other non-human animals, nature and environment.
9 Play: being able to laugh, play and enjoy leisure.
10 Control over one's environment:

   a. Political: have the right to participate in political life.
   b. Material: have rights to seek work and hold property on an equal basis to others.

(Taken from Nussbaum, 2011, pp. 33–34)

While it is acknowledged that a specialist teacher needs to support learners with, for example, progress in reading comprehension, enhanced spelling and improved study skills, it is worth reflecting that education as a process in a child or young person's life is also potentially connected to wider important outcomes vital for their later health, employment, relationships and positive involvement in society.

Research suggests that wider educational outcomes – as captured in some of the ten capabilities above – are even more critical for children with disabilities such as dyslexia than for their typically developing peers (Frederickson and Cline, 2009). Intriguing research also suggests that educators who embody/model positive social and emotional qualities (e.g. apparent 'personal warmth') in their practice seem to encourage enhanced academic performance among their students (Cooper, 2011; Roorda *et al.*, 2011). If accurate, it appears that attention to these wider outcomes has a complementary beneficial effect on the increasingly prized narrower academic outcomes. Given that many children and young people with dyslexia report difficulties with motivation and poor educational experiences (Riddick, 2010), there are clear advantages with adopting this wider emphasis on capabilities being developed by a student, which might not always be clear in the daily emphasis on academic outcomes.

In line with these philosophical discussions, it also worth stating that dyslexia, like any disability, does not have any objective existence 'out there': it is, rather, a shorthand category for a complex pattern of behaviours, strengths and weaknesses which we see in some individuals and which, of course, vary in how they are expressed by each unique individual within the social and political context in which they learn and work. This is an important, potentially limiting notion to keep in mind when thinking about dyslexia in relation to affected children.

Dyslexia and intellectual disability (ID)

In the case studies offered at the start of this book you will recall that Ahmed was referred, initially, on the basis on his increasing difficulty with reading, writing and study. This is what most concerned his educators, at least on one level and alongside worrying behavioural changes which Ahmed presented. Yet, as was highlighted, Ahmed's difficulties with reading, writing and study were small indicators of the much broader, deeper difficulties which he was facing with thought, understanding, attention, language and socialisation. It could be deduced that Ahmed's overall *cognitive functioning* (a term we prefer to 'intelligence') was deteriorating across a number of dimensions.

As a specialist educator practising or aiming to practise with learners who have dyslexia, it is highly likely that you will encounter children, young people or adults who have other co-occurring forms of disability – particularly those which affect cognition and understanding as with Ahmed. These complex cases can confound support for those affected because their needs often cross several professional boundaries and challenge neat categorisation for funding purposes. Understanding what intellectual disability (ID) is can be very helpful in these circumstances, even if it is simply used as a strong basis for referring a student to a psychologist for specialist assessment.

Where the primary focus of the disability is difficulty with cognition, intellect and understanding, then this is typically classified as an ID. This category is still, however, debated and has a highly controversial history within special education (Frederickson and Cline, 2009).

There are several international standards which are used in the diagnosis of ID (also previously referred to, mainly in the US, as 'mental retardation' and, in England, as a general learning difficulty). The most recent fifth edition of the *Diagnostic Statistical Manual* (*DSM 5*) (APA, 2013a) will be referred to in what follows and is an important, internationally used text which facilitates diagnosis of a large range of conditions, syndromes, disorders and disabilities. *DSM 5* is a key, although controversial, resource commonly used by psychologist, psychiatrists, paediatricians and others within the clinical communities (Gornall, 2013).

Guidance releases alongside *DSM 5* in 2013 comments:

> IQ or similar standardized test scores should still be included in an individual's assessment. In DSM-5, intellectual disability is considered to be approximately two standard deviations or more below the population, *which equals an IQ score of about 70 or below.*
>
> (APA, 2013b, our emphasis)

In terms of ID, *DSM 5* refers to an individual's adaptive functioning being affected across three domains, saying that 'diagnosis is made based on the severity of deficits in adaptive functioning' (APA, 2013a, 2013b) and coping across everyday tasks.

- **The conceptual domain** includes skills in language, reading, writing, mathematics, reasoning, knowledge and memory.
- **The social domain** refers to empathy, social judgement, interpersonal communication skills, the ability to make and retain friendships, and similar capacities.
- **The practical domain** centres on self-management in areas such as personal care, job responsibilities, money management, recreation, and organising school and work tasks.

DSM 5 rightly considers that the different domains must be taken into account in assessing the degree of dysfunction this brings to the individual's life before a diagnosis of ID is given. In other words, ID is not determined solely by IQ, but also by the interaction between IQ and the three domains. An IQ score of 70 converts to the second percentile: this means that 98 per cent of age-matched peers who might be tested on the same test would perform at or above this level. The inclusion of the three domains is important. IQ alone does not determine how well a person will do in society. I recently assessed a student following a degree course who had an IQ of 70 with a flat profile across the different subtests and who was not emotionally depressed. She had managed to achieve her academic success through sheer determination, high motivation and sustained effort to build up a conceptual understanding of her subject area and practical skills needed to work in health care. Her social skills were good – although her social life was being sacrificed in order to succeed on her degree course. Similarly low scores were found for *some* people who were working in various professions which had the highest mean IQ in the sample studied (Huang, 2001) (see Table 5.1).

If IQ alone was used to judge whether a person had an ID then, in Huang's study, there would be architects, lawyers and management analysts who would fall into that category. Yet, when the three domains from *DSM 5* are considered, the results of Huang's study make perfect sense as these people would have functional skills in each domain.

Best practice guidance suggests that assessment for ID, should be carried out by a specialist, multidisciplinary team which can include a psychiatrist, psychologist and/or a specialist paediatrician (Haugaard, 2008). Concerns by any adult (parent, educator, school counsellor, SSO, teaching assistant) about a child or young person's intellectual capabilities or adaptive functioning in or around an education setting are sufficient trigger for an assessment on this basis (Haugaard, 2008). This often boils down to concerns about a student's ability to keep up with academic work and tasks set in the classroom. In our experience, a specialist teacher for children with dyslexia is also, from time to time, involved in cases where the intellectual capability and/or intellectual functioning of a learner is a key

Table 5.1 Intelligence and career

Profession	Mean IQ	Min	Max
Mathematical scientists	124.8	98	145
Physicians	124.8	82	145
Lawyers and judges	124.5	73	145
Architects	121.9	69	145
Management analysts	117.6	55	145
Chemists	117.4	83	142

issue of concern. Such cases can be complex, but a specialist educator, like any other professional, should be confident to refer such cases to/seek the involvement of local specialist services.

In much of Australia, these services are described under the umbrella of Disability Services and/or Child and Adolescent Mental Health Services (CAMHS); in other states, territories and across the US/Canada, the analogues there are described under a variety of different names. For example, in the state of California, US, the Department of Developmental Services 'provides services and support to individuals with developmental disabilities'. Regional centres across the state 'will provide additional information about services and, if appropriate, make arrangements to have the child assessed' (California Department of Education, 2004). This state-wide service is funded under national legislation (US Department of Education, 2004). In South Australia (SA), by way of another example, the CAMHS SA team operates across the state and in metropolitan Adelaide. Children with a possible intellectual disability can be initially assessed by the CAMHS psychiatry team and, in many cases, might also be referred to a state Centre for Disability Health which can arrange for specialist assessment around any difficulties which arise from problems with adaptive functioning (South Australian Government, 2013). In England, a similar picture exists, with health, education and social care professionals working together to assess the needs of children and young people up to the age of 25 years (DfE and DoH, 2013a, 2013b).

From another perspective, the literacy difficulties exhibited by those with possible ID, like Ahmed, also often bear some strong resemblance to those experienced by individuals with dyslexia, including, for example, possible difficulties with phonological processing (Conners *et al.*, 2001; Soltani and Roslan, 2013). Research in this area is ongoing and limited, but there is an indication from studies that individuals with ID, like those with dyslexia, often simply require more explicit, structured and carefully considered instruction around developing reading than their typically developing peers (Allor *et al.*, 2010a; Allor *et al.*, 2010b).

Intellectual disability and mental health

If you recall Ahmed's case, you will note that no prior assessment had been conducted of him and that no previous educational records were available to call upon for information about his educational history. Ahmed is a young person, who for varying reasons, has slipped through the cracks in the education system and who now has substantial needs, which include but are much greater than support for his difficulties with reading, writing and study. This is, as you might have gathered, based on a real case which one of the authors worked on and which we wanted to present because it highlighted the complexity of the real lives of children and young people. 'Ahmed' illustrates how what begins as an assessment for dyslexia swiftly becomes a complex case involving:

- a deterioration in the quality of academic study which might, at least initially, indicate a learning difficulty like dyslexia;
- increasing difficulty with oral expressive language;
- increasing social isolation and a loss of/decline in the quality and quantity of relationships with peers;
- cognitive difficulties, including increased difficulty with social understanding and appropriate behaviour, to the extent that they impact on daily life and functioning;
- an emerging possible mental health problem, requiring urgent referral to a specialist agency.

In a thought-provoking paper, Coughlan and Carpenter (2013) note that there is a significant risk of ID co-existing, often unrecognised for years, with a mental health problem which is overshadowed by the presence of the ID label. They also highlight how behaviours by affected children or young people are mistakenly attributed to their intellectual difficulties, but are, in fact, the results of an unrecognised mental health problem. In complex cases such as Ahmed's, this constellation of challenges faced by learners in their everyday (or adaptive) functioning can become synergistic: each co-existing issue can reinforce the other and present a significant overall challenge to their quality of life and chance of enjoying the positive outcomes outlined above in the ten central capabilities. Supporting a student with their reading, writing, spelling, mathematics and study is an important but small part of the wider package of support required here. Such cases often demand a carefully orchestrated multiprofessional approach.

Understanding the underlying concepts (such as adaptive functioning) and practices around the recognition of ID (such as an IQ score of about 70 or below) can assist the specialist educator as they carry out their important role in this team effort.

Reflective questions

Which of Nussbaum's ten capabilities are most relevant in an educational context?

Which of these capabilities was being compromised/negatively affected in Ahmed's case?

What relationship, if any, does cognitive functioning have with dyslexia? How useful is cognitive functioning in terms of thinking about support and/or interventions for children who have dyslexia?

What experience do I have in working with children who have difficulties with cognitive functioning/an ID?

To what extent is Ahmed dysfunctional in each of the three *DSM 5* domains? How does your thinking about this help in deciding if his difficulties would better be classed as a general difficulty (such as ID) or a specific difficulty (such as dyslexia)?

Chapter 6

Dyslexia in higher education

Literacy and dyslexia

In earlier chapters we discussed the fact that, in our society, literacy skills are prized and seen as essential for economic success. Successive western governments have demanded that standards are increased and politically aspirational targets have been set with an expectation that teachers will enable young people to reach these targets. The targets are political and a response to demands from industry and commerce, which increasingly rely on good written communication skills.

Most children learn to read and write fluently as they progress through compulsory education, and an increasing number reach the aspirational targets in both reading and writing. There are some, however, who, despite consistent and appropriate teaching, are unable to master the set of skills associated with communicating through text. Some of these young people will have a functional level of literacy – that is, sufficient skills to meet everyday living needs. Some will not reach this minimum level. Although there may be a number of reasons for failing to acquire literacy skills, many people would consider that the failure to develop reading and/or spelling skills, when there has been good-quality teaching, can be described using the descriptive label 'developmental dyslexia'.[1]

Developmental dyslexia is defined as a difficulty in acquiring the ability to read and/or spell as well as peers despite the provision of adequate tuition. The Rose report on dyslexia defines dyslexia as a 'learning difficulty that primarily affects the skills involved in accurate and fluent word reading and spelling' (Rose, 2009). For school-aged children, there is also a notion of a degree of severity in the difficulty, recognising that some children learn to read and spell more quickly than others and that there will be a continuum of literacy ability from the most able to the least able. Teachers respond to this by providing a graduated response, ranging from differentiated teaching through small group support to intensive individual tuition in literacy.

We have discussed the debate around how bad a pupil needs to be before the descriptive label applies and a diagnosis of dyslexia is given. There is some resistance to pathologising normality and literacy skills; like every other skill, variation is expected in the population between those who have a high degree of ability and those who struggle, exhibiting a normal distribution with most people bunching in the middle. This is comparative and accepts that not everyone will be the same. The diagnosis is then reserved for those people who are well below the mean point. The term 'severe dyslexia' implies literacy skills at least two standard deviations below the mean. This kind of approach to defining dyslexia in school children is also linked to political decisions around providing additional teaching or other supports. In this way, dyslexia is seen as a comparative condition in which the learner is compared to other learners in the same context. In schools, we are comparing an individual learner to a wider population of learners, stretching from those with very complex and severe learning difficulties to those who are very able. Should we make the same comparison in universities by comparing to the whole adult population or should we compare students to a student population? We would argue that the latter comparison is the one to make. There is an interesting consequence of making this decision. The normal distribution of abilities found in students is likely to be higher than that found in the wider population. This can mean that a student who was assessed as a child and not found to be dyslexic might, on assessment at university, be diagnosed with dyslexia. The label is being used in a relativistic way to describe the student's abilities in literacy with respect to a reference group of other students. This makes sense because the work environment and literacy demands on the student are much higher in an academic setting than in the wider world of adulthood where there is a considerable variation in literacy skills.

Another approach to thinking about dyslexia has been one that relies on the correlation between intelligence and literacy skills. This is based on the assumption that some people find learning easier than others and seem to be good at everything that they are asked to do. In short, they are more intelligent than those who struggle with learning. This means that we can use intelligence as a predictor of literacy skills and look for unusual differences between predicted skills and actual skills. The term 'severe dyslexia' would now refer to a large degree of underperformance and is now an ipsative comparison rather than a comparison between one individual and the rest of the population. In school children, this approach to defining dyslexia solely on the basis of a discrepancy has been rejected. This is partly because there can be many reasons why a child fails to learn to read or spell.

Some authors see all literacy difficulties in children as deserving the diagnosis dyslexia, irrespective of causation. This would include children with profound and multiple learning difficulties, children with severe learning difficulties, children with language difficulties, children with behaviour difficulties etc. There would be no attempt to differentially diagnose dyslexia; this makes sense when considering that the approaches used to teach literacy to dyslexic and non-dyslexic children are the same. It is a pragmatic argument based on pedagogy. Other authors, and the Code of Practice for Special Educational Needs, prefer a differential diagnosis and define dyslexia as a specific learning difficulty (DfES, 2001; Riddick, 2001). However, the two terms are not synonymous and there are other types of specific learning difficulty (such as dyspraxia, autism and ADHD). For university students, there is a need for a differential diagnosis; this requirement is partly due to the need to carry out a protocol that is acceptable to funders who provide additional support. In England, this would be in the form of Disabled Students' Allowance (DSA) (SpLD Assessment Standards Committee, 2010; SpLD Test Evaluation Committee, 2009). In 1998/99, 24 per cent of higher education students with a recognised disability had a specific learning difficulty (Konur, 2002). Not all of these would be given a diagnosis of dyslexia; other data suggests that around 15 per cent of students in 1994/95 were dyslexic (Riddell and Weedon, 2006).This means that the assessment must rule out other difficulties through a differential diagnosis that explores alternative explanations for the observed literacy difficulties and any unexpected discrepancies in performance. It also suggests that, to be meaningful to the student, the term 'dyslexia' should be used as the best descriptive label for their condition.

Another way of defining dyslexia is based on the assumption that reading and writing are complex skills that require many areas of the brain to function well. The evidence for this is drawn from studies involving adults who have acquired dyslexia, from post mortem studies of known dyslexics and, from neurological studies using brain imaging of healthy dyslexic participants. This has led to dyslexia being defined as a complex neurological condition affecting around 4 per cent of the population (Carroll and Iles, 2006). The implication from this is that dyslexia will have many features and not only affect literacy skills. Even when poor literacy skills are overcome (sometimes referred to as compensated dyslexia), the other features will still be present. These difficulties may include: slow processing speed, poor working memory, poor organisation, poor attentional control, poor phonological processing. Not all individuals with dyslexia will have all of these problems. There are other overlapping conditions that can lead to the same cognitive weaknesses (e.g. ADHD, ASD, SLI, DCD, ideational dyspraxia).

Assessing dyslexia at university

In higher education, we are faced with students who have sufficient literacy skills to be able to pass the required examinations at GCE A Level (some with special examination arrangements), but who cannot read or spell as accurately and fluently as their peers. Their degree of difficulty in the wider population would often go unnoticed, but within the university setting of high expectations around literacy, their literacy skills lead to a degree of dysfunction; that is, there is 'a failure to meet the demands of particular social expectations of literacy' (Collinson and Penketh, 2010, p. 9). This is an important point that we have already made, since it emphasises the need to compare like with like. We need to compare the literacy skills of a given student with the literacy skills of the general student population and the expected levels of literacy performance to be able to cope with learning and assessment tasks. This means that there will be students who are assessed at university who are found to be dyslexic who have not been diagnosed in the past because their levels of literacy skills are comparable to the wider adult population but below the predicted levels for their given ability. One way to test this to look for a discrepancy between predicted and observed levels of literacy, based on intelligence.

However, some authors argue that dyslexia is fundamentally a language processing disorder affecting phonological awareness and phonological processing (Hatcher *et al.*, 2002). Using this argument, they have found that dyslexia can be correctly diagnosed 95.7 per cent of the time using a protocol involving only four subtests: spelling, non-word reading, digit span (a measure of short-term memory capacity) and writing speed (Hatcher *et al.*, 2002). This narrow approach does not allow the psychologist to take into account the neurological and cognitive models of information processing so that a differential diagnosis can be made. For example, developmental co-ordination disorder (dyspraxia) has been found to overlap with dyslexia in many university students (Kirby *et al.*, 2008a; Kirby *et al.*, 2008b). There are other limitations to this narrow assessment protocol. For example, having only four subtests means that there is a heavy weighting on spelling scores, yet it has been found that there is a wide variation in spelling ability in undergraduate dyslexic students, with misspelling rates between 1 per cent and 31 per cent of words (Riddick *et al.*, 1999). Measuring short-term memory capacity may give some insight into the phonological loop; however, it does not provide useful measures of how attentional resources are allocated in working memory (referred to as executive function). The solution is to use a protocol that is efficient in terms of assessment time, yet is not too restrictive to allow for dyslexia to be diagnosed successfully in students for whom the underlying cause is not limited to a language processing disorder. Such an assessment should allow for differential diagnoses and allow compensated dyslexia to be explored. The models for the assessment should be derived from cognitive, neurological and developmental psychology as well as drawing upon normative data for comparisons with the relevant peer group.

Task analysis and consideration of the types of skills that students need to succeed in higher education can inform the assessment process. For example, the skills involved in writing can be grouped into transcription skills and executive skills. Transcription skills include handwriting skills – fluency and letter formation – and spelling skills. Executive skills are related to the executive function of working memory and include planning what to write, monitoring what has been written and the development of the prose, reviewing, revising, organising ideas and paragraphs, and switching attention (Connelly *et al.*, 2006). During a writing task, the working memory of a dyslexic student is likely to become overloaded with the demands of the linguistic task (Connelly *et al.*, 2006). The quality of the writing is likely to be further reduced because the reading vocabularies of dyslexic students are less extensive compared with non-dyslexic students (Connelly *et al.*, 2006).

The assessment also needs to explore emotional responses to the demands of higher education. For example, one study has found that dyslexic students experience higher levels of academic, social and reading-situational anxiety than non-dyslexic peers, and a negative correlation between levels of anxiety and reading rate (Carroll and Iles, 2006). Levels of social and academic stress are reported to be higher among dyslexic students than non-dyslexic students. Dyslexic students also reported lower levels of social support, thought to be because they want to hide their dyslexia and be seen to be coping by themselves (Heiman and Kariv, 2004).

Students entering higher education in England may have had assessments undertaken when they were at school or college. From September 2014, the local authority in the area in which they live has responsibility for maintaining any Education and Health Care Plans for disabled students with complex needs up to the age of 25 (DfE and DoH, 2013b). However, many students with dyslexia are unlikely to fall under these arrangements and local authorities will provide them with guidance and advice on securing social care and Disabled Students' Allowance (DSA) (Disability Rights UK, 2014). Each university in England has their own disability support service, which can advise students on how to be assessed for DSA if this has not been done already. For students who think that they may be dyslexic, this will also include a referral to an educational psychologist. In higher education, this assessment tends to rely on a single assessment following an agreed set of guidelines (DfES, 2005a; SpLD Assessment Standards

Committee, 2010; SpLD Test Evaluation Committee, 2009). The difficulty with one-off psychometric assessments is that there are many factors that can influence performance; on any particular day, the degree to which these are evident may affect the score on a given subtest (Faulkner and Blyth, 1996). Psychologists working in school settings can overcome this limitation by carrying out the assessment over time and can draw on other evidence that allows the validity of the psychometric assessment to be verified and alternative hypotheses arising from ipsative profiles to be explored. The psychologist conducting a clinical assessment does not have the same luxury. However, the interpretation can be improved through a number of approaches:

- Quickly settling the student and developing rapport so that test anxiety is reduced. This includes explaining the nature of the assessment and that it is normal not to be able to answer all items used in the assessment. It has also been pointed out that dyslexia gets worse when a student is placed under stress (Sanderson-Mann and McCandless, 2005).
- Taking time during the assessment and allowing breaks if the student appears to need it, while also moving fluidly from one subtest to the next.
- Ensuring multiple measures of reading skills and writing skills (e.g. reading accuracy on single words, decoding of pseudo-words, reading accuracy with passages of text, reading comprehension, reading fluency and rate, spelling single words, spelling in extended writing, writing fluency, writing organisation and structure).
- Making use of screening assessments carried out by a trained tutor prior to the psychologist carrying out the psychometric assessment and comparing with similar measures used during the assessment. Financial pressures on universities may mean that these pre-screening measures are not available.
- Carrying out a comprehensive cognitive assessment that goes beyond simply measuring IQ and includes measures associated with dyslexia (e.g. processing speed, working memory), taking into account specific weaknesses in deciding the most appropriate measure of intellectual ability (e.g. reporting General Ability Index scores instead of Full Scale IQ).
- Making observations of cognitive processing behaviours (e.g. noting word-finding difficulties, organisational difficulties, co-ordination difficulties, difficulties with maintaining and directing attentional focus and control).

- Using the ipsative profile of subtest scores to look for significant levels of uneven performance and comparing this to clinical observations of student cognitive processing behaviour to generate hypotheses that can then be explored through discussion with the student about their experiences of potential difficulties in everyday life. Part of the discussion should then move onto exploring practical solutions to any difficulties experienced so that potential reasonable adjustments can be made.

Social model of disability

There has been a growth in the number of students diagnosed with dyslexia attending university (Connelly *et al.*, 2006; Hatcher *et al.*, 2002). This was first noted as far back as 1995, when a massive increase in requests for psychological assessment was reported (Faulkner and Blyth, 1996). In 1996, 1 per cent of all students in higher education were diagnosed as being dyslexic (Lockley, 2002); by 1999, this had increased to 3.8 per cent (Heiman and Kariv, 2004). Between 2000 and 2004, the number of diagnosed dyslexic students attending university doubled (Kirby *et al.*, 2008a). Data collected by the Higher Education Statistics Agency reveals how the number of students identified with dyslexia has changed over the last 20 years (HESA, 2014).

The HESA data reveals a lower number of dyslexic students than the previous studies suggested. This may be because this data is all first-year students at all levels of study. The general pattern is in agreement with increasing numbers of students identified as being dyslexic (Figure 6.1). According to HESA's data, in actual numbers of first-year students starting courses at any level who were dyslexic rose from 2,359 in 1994–95 to 37,615 in 2011–12. This is almost 16 times the number of students who required an assessment of dyslexia. However, the percentage of first-year students who were identified as dyslexic in 2011–12 was about 4.3 per cent compared to estimates of between 10–17 per cent of all adults who have dyslexia (BDA, Undated; Dyslexia Research Institute, 2014; PBS Parents, 2014).

The HESA data also shows that the fraction of the student population that had any disability (including dyslexia) continued to rise. However, further analysis shows that the increase in disabled students is largely due to the number of students identified as dyslexic and the proportion of disabled students with dyslexia increases from 15 per cent to almost half of all disabled university students (Figure 6.2).

There is a temptation to think about dyslexia from a medical model, that is to say that a person is disabled through a set of cognitive deficits. The clinical assessment carried out by a specialist reinforces this perspective.

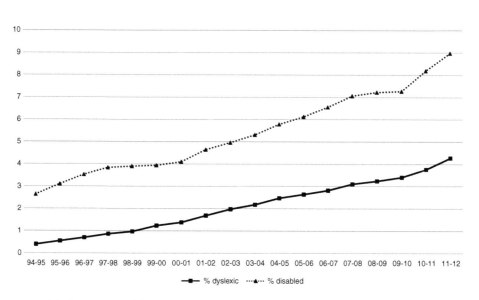

Figure 6.1 Percentage of first-year students across all courses who were identified as dyslexic and disabled.

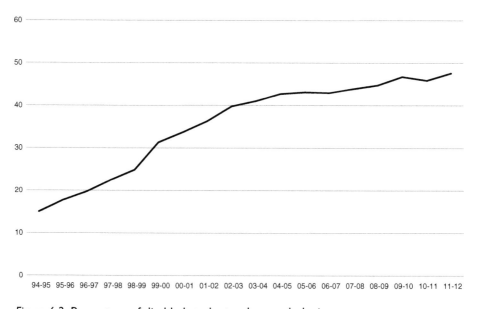

Figure 6.2 Percentage of disabled students who are dyslexic.

In this context, dyslexia is seen as a disability; one of the uses of the psychological assessment is to enable dyslexic students to claim DSA. Premium funding has been provided to universities since 1999–2000 on the basis of DSA that has been claimed; this has been criticised as reinforcing the view that the disability is a 'within-student' difficulty (Riddell *et al.*, 2007; Vickermana and Blundell, 2010).

Thought about in this way, the increase in dyslexic students attending university is problematic because the students will not be able to cope with the literacy demands placed upon them, which are well within the capabilities of their non-dyslexic peers. This may account for the lower representation of dyslexics among the student population compared to the wider adult population. This was evidenced during the 1990s, when one concern was that many students were applying for courses for which they were cognitively unsuitable, particularly as many dyslexic students were dropping out of education at the end of the first year of their degree course (Faulkner and Blyth, 1996). Potentially, this could have got worse with political moves to encourage more young people to attend university. With widening participation in education during the beginning of this century, there has been an increase in the number of students attending university who otherwise would have been under-represented or disenfranchised (Collinson and Penketh, 2010). However, like any disability, dyslexia is not an absolute – it is a relative construct. The extent to which a relative difficulty with literacy or slow processing speed or working memory difficulties impacts on study can be mediated by the social context in which the study takes place. That is to say, the same levels of ability can have differing degrees of disability in different institutions (or even in different parts of the same institution). This is because the disability has an environmental and social component (Riddell and Weedon, 2006). The cognitive impairments are turned into a disability through the negative attitudes of the social setting (Riddick, 2001). The social model of disability argues that a lack of responsiveness by educationalists leads to students with dyslexia failing to achieve in higher education (Collinson and Penketh, 2010).

Over the years, there have been various pieces of legislation that attempt to make environments less disabling. Part IV of the Disability Discrimination Act (HMSO, 1995), as amended by the Special Educational Needs and Disability Act (HMSO, 2001), required reasonable adjustments to be made to allow people with identified disabilities to be able to participate in education. For instance, institutions cannot discriminate against admitting a student to a course on the grounds of literacy (or dyslexia) if the student is sufficiently intellectually bright to undertake the course (Konur, 2002; Sanderson-Mann and McCandless, 2005). The Disability Discrimination Act also required reasonable steps to be taken to ensure that a disabled student was not disadvantaged unfairly in comparison to a student who was not disabled. The Quality Assurance Agency for Higher Education expresses this more clearly, saying that assessment and examination policies should ensure that students with disabilities have the same opportunities to demonstrate learning outcomes as peers (Lockley, 2002; Vickermana and Blundell, 2010). The Equality Act 2010 (HMSO, 2010) replaced previous legislation; universities retain responsibility to make reasonable adjustments for students (and employees) in a number of categories of disability, including mental health.

However, the adaptation of teaching or examination processes presents a challenge to higher education's idea of absolute standards (Riddell and Weedon, 2006). One of the issues surrounding diagnoses of dyslexia in higher education is the principle that such a diagnosis should lead to reasonable adjustments without providing the student with an unfair advantage over peers. From the students' point of view, in a very competitive employment market where the class of degree makes a difference, it would seem wise to explore every potential avenue for increasing examination grade marks. If the student has a literacy difficulty or cognitive processing difficult that can be reasonably adjusted for (for instance, by allowing additional time in examinations), then it makes sense to ask for an assessment and to seek out these adjustments. Part of the debate around assessment in higher education centres on the impression that some students would like to cheat the system by asking for adjustments that are not necessary, which, if given, would lead to an unfair advantage. The temptation to do this is increased when there are additional incentives in the form of Disabled Students' Allowance. This is not a new debate and has been a feature of all public examinations for some considerable time. The circle is squared a little by Pumfrey, who points out that reasonable adjustments must take into account 'the maintenance of academic standards; costs and resources; health and safety requirements; and the practicality and effectiveness of the adjustment' (Pumfrey, 2008, p. 38).

Pumfrey's clarification is helpful when thinking about courses where 'fitness to practice' is an issue. For example, there is a tension between making reasonable adjustments for students following courses in clinical professions and ensuring that patient safety is not compromised (Sanderson-Mann and McCandless, 2005). The student must be able to keep proper records and administer medicines safely in order to demonstrate professional competence; however, the assessment methods for determining this should not be discriminatory. This could be as simple as allowing more time so that practical strategies can be implemented, for example, allowing the student to make use of hyper-vigilance and compulsive behaviours such as checking and rechecking drug calculations and rereading paperwork (Morris and Turnbull, 2007b).

Disclosure of dyslexia in clinical settings potentially improves support for the student nurse and increases aspects of patient safety; however, many student nurses are fearful of the stigma of making such a disclosure (Morris and Turnbull, 2007a). This is also true of the wider student population, who are encouraged to disclose disabilities on their UCAS application forms (Disability Rights UK, 2014). There is some evidence that, despite changes in legislation, some students do not disclose disabilities that could lead to increased support for a variety of reasons, including stigmatisation and fear of not being offered a place on their desired course of study (Vickermana and Blundell, 2010).

One way of dealing with this and increasing participation of dyslexic pupils is to improve teaching more generally in universities by removing potential barriers to learning for all students. Such an approach follows the logic that teaching methods could be seen as potentially disabling for some students; attempts to anticipate these problems before they arise could minimise this. In an ideal world, such a move would allow all students to participate fully and it would reduce the need for individual assessments. Examples showing the difference between the medical model and the social model are given below.

- The medical model requires individuals to be assessed to show that their processing speed or reading fluency is lower than peers so that they can have extended library loans (a reasonable adjustment). The social model understands that people are different and that time constraints are disadvantageous to some students. A different approach follows and course texts are obtained in an electronic form so that there is no need for the library to recall texts or limit the loan time in order for more students to access them. Students can study the electronic version as often as they need to do so. Students who need more time to make sense of the text can manage the time themselves without worrying about returning a scarce resource.
- Assessments carried out of individuals using the medical model show that they find it hard to follow course handouts in lectures. A reasonable adjustment requires that lecturers allow students who have been assessed to access the course handouts in advance so that they can pre-read the handouts and know the structure of the lecture before the lecture occurs. In the social model, understanding that many students would benefit from knowing the structure of the lecture in advance enables the university to develop its virtual learning environment where key texts, links to multimedia presentations and course handouts are stored for access by all students before the lecture. The lecture itself is automatically recorded and uploaded as a blog so that students can revisit the lecture to hear key arguments and discussion.

Conclusions

There are an increasing number of students gaining entry into higher education. There are some students who are not dyslexic but who want to be assessed so that they benefit from different support systems, reasonable adjustments and DSA. There are some students who are dyslexic but are reluctant to be assessed and miss out on these arrangements. Rather than thinking about dyslexia as a disability of the student, we could use the social model of disability to consider dyslexia to be a disability that can be removed through a change in teaching and assessment practice.

If this is done globally, then the number of students requiring psychological assessment that differentiates between the different types of specific learning difficulty could be reduced as the environment takes into account variation in levels of literacy, processing speed, working memory, attentional control and organisational skills. This can be done in a way that does not lead to a compromise in academic standards or produce professionals that are not fit to practice.

This kind of approach has started to be introduced into schools, with an inclusive ideology referred to as 'dyslexia-friendly'; there are many slight changes that can be made to improve learning and teaching (Squires, 2001, 2002, 2004, 2010; Squires and McKeown, 2006). The same approach may be employed in universities by considering policies around teaching and learning, and training lecturers in teaching approaches that are socially inclusive.

Note

1 Dyslexia can occur in later life through brain injury or degeneration; this is referred to as 'acquired dyslexia'.

Conclusion

Dyslexia, the bio-psycho-social model and inclusion?

This book began by asking you to consider three case studies (John, Ahmed and Lara) which illustrated some of the key issues tackled therein. We hope that these also disclosed some of the rich complexity which a specialist teacher will encounter in their daily practice with students (of all kinds) who present with dyslexia. Real individuals are, as you might gather, often imperfectly accommodated by systems and ideas which call on generalisations and fixed categories.

What we have, therefore, tried to convey in this book is that the nature of dyslexia is complex and that no two individuals with dyslexia will experience it in quite the same way. The bio-psycho-social model – often used in clinical psychology to show the interaction between different levels of organisation – might be useful in accommodating the diversity we see among those affected by dyslexia. This model acknowledges how bio-psycho-social dimensions interact in shaping individuals' *experience of dyslexia* and also inform their *presentation* of dyslexia (behaviours or factors attributed to dyslexia). In the context of dyslexia, it encompasses:

- **The biological** components of dyslexia, such as the neural pathways and areas of brain function: discussed in the Introduction to this book and in Chapter 2.
- **The psychological** components of dyslexia, including reading skills, motivation, self-concept, self-esteem, behaviour; these were highlighted in Chapter 2, Chapter 4 and Chapter 5.
- **The social** components of dyslexia, including the agendas at play in educational systems and the political environment in which dyslexia is recognised, defined and used. The way in which society 'constructs' dyslexia as a condition that needs treatment and is worthy of intervention can be seen as a helpful, as well as unhelpful, part of this social component. This process was raised in our book's Introduction and in Chapter 6.

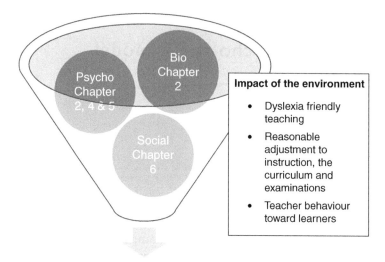

The experience of dyslexia

Figure C.1 The bio-psycho-social-environment model.

The area which is less clear in the overall bio-psycho-social model is that of the role played by environment. The 'environment', in this context, includes the extent to which the learning, examining and working environments can be adjusted, as discussed in Chapter 6 in the context of higher education.

Understanding how these all link together can help the educator provide the right kind of teaching and learning so that the student has a positive experience of dyslexia. Failing to understand these issues will often lead to a hostile teaching environment in which the dyslexic student struggles to survive and has a negative experience of dyslexia – with a host of probable negative outcomes for those affected. This argument is graphically expressed by Figure C.1, which sets the issues within the context of this book.

Dyslexia, inclusion and teaching

We have suggested throughout that this text, therefore, does not position itself as a categorical 'how to' guide, rather hoping to provoke critical questions from you ('why we should') on the topics presented. We hope that this book has provided a thoughtful context for the general principles underlying 'structured, sequential, multi-sensory teaching' (BDA, 2012), which might inform a 'structured, sequential, multi-sensory teaching programme to meet individual needs' (BDA, 2013). Indeed, the reflective questions given at the end of the case studies presented in our book's Introduction might act of as a starting point for a programme designed to support the unique needs of each individual.

Chapters 1 to 6 explored, in further detail, some of the points which each case illustrated and which, directly or indirectly, affect the design, implementation and evaluation of programmes of support or practice more generally. Lara, for example, exemplifies many of the self-remediated, often highly motivated students we might encounter post-school at university/in higher study who also present with dyslexia – issues discussed in Chapter 6. John's challenges – his motivation at school; with maintaining a positive sense of academic self-esteem; and with his conduct – were addressed in the context of behaviour in Chapter 4. Ahmed's case was reflected in the issues outlined in Chapter 5, in light of the topics of mental health and the assessment of intelligence. Each of these constellations of needs should inform exactly what is designed into any programme of support for each individual.

A brief consideration of real individuals and a reflection on what a 'structured, sequential, multi-sensory teaching programme to meet individual needs' actually is points, we think, towards the conclusion that it is simply another way of describing very high-quality teaching. The bio-psycho-social model, discussed a moment ago, can add something unique to this insight: it suggests that helping to engender a positive experience of dyslexia in an accommodating learning environment is probably a core marker of high-quality teaching for those affected by dyslexia.

In turn, this enabling environment can be helpfully informed by theoretical frameworks, such as the bio-psycho-social model, which recognise dyslexia across the biological, psychological and social domains. Indeed, we might suspect that a phenomenon as varied and complex as dyslexia can only be understood by such a comprehensive frame.

Here, then, is a technical expression of our argument in conclusion to this book:

The bio-psycho-social model *facilitates a* recognition of the individual's experience of dyslexia across bio-psycho-social domains which *informs* an enabling learning environment, engendering a positive experience of dyslexia, thereby creating the *best* (optimal) conditions to design and to enact a structured, sequential, multisensory teaching programme to best meet individual needs.

This highlights the complex question of what distinguishes a specialist teacher from a general or non-specialist teacher for students presenting with dyslexia. This is a major question for ongoing, international research into teacher education, teacher development and professional effectiveness (Forlin, 2012). This potentially controversial question is, for the most part, outside of the remit of this book, but it is worth addressing in a more limited, practical way for our reader. The following section gives an outline of what might characterise a specialist educator practising with students who present with dyslexia. It is intended as a general outline, in addition to the specific skills and knowledge delineated, for example, by the BDA and discussed in this book's Introduction.

Professional profile of a specialist teacher (dyslexia/LD)

He or she most probably:

1 collaborates extensively with other professionals outside of education (psychologists, social workers, clinicians) in supporting students with dyslexia, along with other co-occurring disabilities affecting learning;
2 has a confident understanding of core facets of professional roles and relevant practices from other disciplines, such as psychology;
3 leads professional learning for colleagues around legislation, policy, research and practice and in relation to dyslexia;
4 orchestrates (often complex) support for children with disabilities or additional needs, including work with families where appropriate;
5 is an experienced and successful educator before becoming/at the same time as being a specialist educator;
6 is conversant with concepts and knowledge used in assessment of dyslexia, including, for example, the principles and practice of psychometric testing;
7 has a thorough knowledge of custom, practices and systems used in relation to students with dyslexia in their setting/educational area;
8 practises within the wider framework of inclusion, enabling that student the same opportunities to learn, progress and achieve as their non-disabled peers.

Across the UK, US, Canada, New Zealand and Australia the need for a specialist educator role has been increasingly reinforced by policy or national legislation which refers to dyslexia. In many cases the professional role described in this book has been (financially and professionally) validated by legislation. In New Zealand, for example, the Education Act (1989) and Human Rights Act (1994) both guarantee a free education for all children with a disability with opportunity to attend a local school (see Ministry of

Education, New Zealand, 2013). In the UK the Special Educational Code of Practice (2001) refers specifically to meeting the full educational needs of students (in primary or secondary education) affected by dyslexia; and the Equality Act (2010) placed the onus on universities to make reasonable adjustments at all levels for students and employees affected by disability. In the US IDEA legislation (2004, 2009) mandates and legally underpins the delivery and evaluation of education, across all states and territories, to students with a disability, including those specifically described as having a reading disability and/or dyslexia. In Australia, at state and federal policy level, a variety of drivers for change have increasingly conspired to support the role for a specialist teacher in education settings and which has been described by this book. Influential factors for policy development include: the Melbourne Declaration (MCEECDYA, 2008); the emergence of the Australian Professional Standards for Teachers (2012); the emergence of an Australian National Curriculum; and most recently an 'agenda for nation action' (Australian Government, 2013) focussing on the educational welfare and achievement of students who present with dyslexia. This movement, in English-speaking countries, in favouring the role of a specialist educator for students affected by dyslexia is likely to have wider implications. Emerging nations such as China, India, Indonesia, Mexico and the Philippines look in varying degrees to English-speaking countries when thinking about how they might develop their own educational systems and enhance the inclusion of students with a disability (Forlin, 2012).

A final reference to inclusion is a fitting end to this book. Countries across the globe are now signatories to a range of binding international legislation by the United Nations/UNESCO which underpins the rights and aspirations of students to an inclusive, high-quality education at primary and secondary (high school) level (United Nations, 2006). Meeting the needs of students with disabilities, including their inclusion in the range of opportunities offered to their non-disabled peers, is explicitly addressed in this legislation (United Nations, 2006, Article 24 (2b)).

Whatever the difficulties with precisely defining inclusion and with carrying it out in practice (Forlin, 2012; Armstrong and Squires, 2012), the specialist educator described in this book is a key professional with a clear remit to enable an array of positive outcomes for students they support. They (and you) are potentially an agent of significant *positive change* in our public education systems around inclusion and in favour of social justice: this is in accordance with the principles set out by this historic, international legislation.

References

Adey, P., and Dillon, J. (eds) (2012). *Bad Education: Debunking Myths in Education*. Maidenhead: Open University Press.

Agnew, J. A., Dom, C., and Eden, G. G. (2004). Effect of intensive training on auditory processing and reading skills. *Brain and Language*, 88, 21–25.

Ainscow, M., and Miles, S. (2008). Making education inclusive for all: where next? *Prospects*, 38, 15–34.

Alexander-Passe, N. (2012). *Dyslexia and Depression: The Hidden Sorrow*. New York: Nova.

Allor, J. H., Mathes, P. G., Roberts, J. K., Cheatham, J. P., and Champlin, T. M. (2010a). Comprehensive reading instruction for students with intellectual disabilities: findings from the first three years of a longitudinal study. *Psychology in the Schools*, 47(5), 445–466.

Allor, J. H., Mathes, P. G., Roberts, J. K., Jones, F., and Champlin, T. M. (2010b). Teaching students with moderate intellectual disabilities to read: an experimental examination of a comprehensive reading intervention. *Education and Training in Developmental Disabilities*, 45(1), 3.

Alloway, T. P. (2011). *Improving Working Memory: Supporting Students Learning*. London: Sage.

APA (2013a). *Diagnostic and Statistical Manual of Mental Disorders* (5th edn). Arlington, VA: American Psychiatric Association.

APA (2013b). *Intellectual Disability: Factsheet*. New York: American Psychiatric Association.

APS (2007). *Code of Ethics*. Melbourne, Victoria: Australian Psychological Society.

Armstrong, D. (2013). Educator perceptions of children who present with social, emotional and behavioural difficulties: a literature review with implications for recent educational policy in England and internationally. *International Journal of Inclusive Education*. doi: 10.1080/13603116.2013.823245, 18(7), 731–745.

Armstrong, D., and Humphrey, N. (2009). Reactions to a diagnosis of dyslexia among students entering further education: development of the 'resistance-accommodation' model. *British Journal of Special Education*, 36, 95–102. doi: 10.1111/j.1467-8578.2008.00408.x

Armstrong, D., and Squires, G. (eds) (2012). *Contemporary Issues in Special Educational Needs: Considering the Whole Child*. Maidenhead: Open University Press/McGraw-Hill Education.

Atkinson, C., and Squires, G. (2011). Educational psychologists and therapeutic intervention: promoting positive mental health. Paper presented at the 3rd European Network for Social and Emotional Competence in Children. University of Manchester.

Australian Government (2005). *National Inquiry into the Teaching of Literacy*. Canberra: Department of Education, Science and Training.

Australian Government (2013). *Response to Recommendations of the Dyslexia Working Party Report: 'Helping people with dyslexia: a national action agenda'*. Canberra: Department of Families, Housing, Community Services and Indigenous Affairs.

Baddeley, A. D., and Hitch, G. J. (1974). Working memory. In G. H. Bower (ed.), *The Psychology of Learning and Motivation* (Vol. 8, pp. 47–90). New York: Academic Press.

Baumeister, R. F., Campbell, J. D., Krueger, J. I., and Vohs, K. D. (2003). Does high self-esteem cause better performance, interpersonal success, happiness, or healthier lifestyles? *Psychological Science in the Public Interest*, 4, 1–44.

BDA (2012). *Criteria for Recognition of Teachers and other Professionals with Specialist Training*. Bracknell: British Dyslexia Association.

BDA (Undated). British Dyslexia Association: About Us. Retrieved 21 January 2014, from http://www.bdadyslexia.org.uk/about-us.html

Beck, A. T., and Emery, G. (1979). *Cognitive Therapy of Anxiety and Phobic Disorders*. Philadelphia: Center for Cognitive Therapy.

Beck, A. T., Emery, G., and Greenberg, R. (1985). *Anxiety Disorders and Phobias: A Cognitive Perspective*. New York: Basic Books.

Beck, A. T., Freeman, E., and Associates. (1990). *Cognitive Therapy of Personality Disorders*. London: Guilford Press.

Beck, A. T., Rush, A., Shaw, B., and Emery, G. (1979). *Cognitive Therapy of Depression*. New York: Guilford Press.

Bell, S. (2013). Professional development for specialist teachers and assessors of students with literacy difficulties/dyslexia: 'to learn how to assess and support children with dyslexia'. *Journal of Research in Special Educational Needs*, 13(1), 104–113.

Beneventi, H., Tøønnessen, F. E., Ersland, L., and Hugdahl, K. (2010). Working memory deficit in dyslexia: behavioral and fMRI evidence. *International Journal of Neuroscience*, 120(1), 51–59.

Berkeley, S., Bender, W. N., Peaster, L. G., and Saunders, L. (2009). Implementation of response to intervention a snapshot of progress. *Journal of Learning Disabilities*, 42(1), 85–95.

Binet, A., and Simon, T. (1916). (1905/1916). Méthodes nouvelles pour le diagnostic du niveau intellectuel des anormaux [New methods for the diagnosis of the intellectual level of subnormals]. *L'Année Psychologique*, 11, 191–244 [English translation] In E. S. Kite (ed.), *The Development of Intelligence in Children*. Vineland, NJ: Publications of the Training School at Vineland.

Blatchford, P., Bassett, P., Brown, P., Koutsoubou, M., Martin, C., Russell, A., and Webster, R., with Rubie-Davies, C. (2009a). *Deployment and Impact of*

Support Staff in Schools: Results from Wave 2, Strand 2. London: Department for Children, Schools and Families.

Blatchford, P., Bassett, P., Brown, P., Martin, C., Russell, A., and Webster, R. (2009b). *Deployment and Impact of Support Staff Project: RB148.* London: Department for Children, Schools and Families.

Blomert, L., and Willems, G. (2010). Is there a causal link from a phonological awareness deficit to reading failure in children at familial risk for dyslexia? *Dyslexia*, 16(4), 300–317.

Bond, J., Coltheart, M., Connell, T., Firth, N., Hardy, M., and Nayton, M. (2010). *Helping People with Dyslexia: A National Action Agenda. Report from the Dyslexia Working Party Submitted to the Parliamentary Secretary for Disabilities and Children's Services.* Australia.

BPS (1999). *Dyslexia, Literacy and Psychological Assessment. Report of a Working Party of the Division of Educational and Child Psychology.* Leicester: British Psychological Society.

BPS (2009). *Code of Ethics and Conduct.* Leicester: British Psychological Society.

Bradley, L., and Bryant, P. E. (1978). Difficulties in auditory organisation as a possible cause of reading backwardness. *Nature*, 271, 746–747.

Bradley, R., Danielson, L., and Doolittle, J. (2005). Response to Intervention. *Journal of Learning Disabilities*, 38(6), 485–486.

Bryant, P. E., and Bradley, L. (1983). Categorising sounds and learning to read: a causal connection. *Nature*, 301, 419–521.

Burchardt, T. (2010). Capabilities and disability: the capabilities framework and the social model of disability. *Disability and Society*, 19(7), 735–751.

Burden, R. (2005). *Dyslexia and Self-Concept: Seeking a Dyslexic Identity.* London: Whurr.

Burden, R. (2008). Is dyslexia necessarily associated with negative feelings of self-worth? *Dyslexia*, 14, 188–196.

Burden, R., and Burdett, J. (2005). Factors associated with successful learning in pupils with dyslexia: a motivational analysis. *British Journal of Special Education*, 32(2), 100–104.

Burden, R., and Burdett, J. (2007). What's in a name? Students with dyslexia: their use of metaphor in making sense of their disability. *British Journal of Special Education*, 34(2), 77–82.

Cajkler, W., Sage, R., Tennant, G., Tiknaz, Y., Tucker, S., and Taylor, C. (2007). *Working with Adults. How Training and Professional Development Activities Impact on Teaching Assistants' Classroom Practice (1988–2006).* London: EPPI-Centre.

California Department of Education. (2004). *Reasons for Concern that Your Child or a Child in Your Care May Need Special Help.* Sacramento: California Department of Education.

Carroll, J. M., and Iles, J. E. (2006). An assessment of anxiety levels in dyslexic students in higher education. *British Journal of Educational Psychology*, 76(3), 651–662.

Carroll, J. M., Bowyer-Crane, C., Duff, F. J., Hulme, C., and Snowling, M. J. (2011). Theoretical framework: foundations of learning to read. In J. M. Carroll, C. Bowyer-Crane, F. J. Duff, C. Hulme and M. J. Snowling, *Developing Language and Literacy: Effective Intervention in the Early Years* (pp. 1–16). Oxford: Wiley-Blackwell.

Charlton, T. (1992). Giving access to the national curriculum by working on the self. In K. Jones and T. Charlton (eds), *Learning Difficulties in Primary Classrooms: Delivering the Whole Curriculum*. London: Routledge.

Cleary, T. J., Callan, G. L., and Zimmerman, B. J. (2012). Assessing self-regulation as a cyclical, context-specific phenomenon: overview and analysis of SRL microanalytic protocols. *Education Research International*, vol. 2012, article ID 428639. doi:10.1155/2012/428639

Cohen, L., Manion, L., and Morrison, K. (2007). *Research Methods in Education*. Oxford: Routledge.

Collinson, C., and Penketh, C. (2010). 'Sit in the corner and don't eat the crayons': postgraduates with dyslexia and the dominant 'lexic' discourse. *Disability and Society*, 25(1), 7–19.

Cone, J. D. (1997). Issues in functional analysis in behavioral assessment. *Behaviour Research Therapy*, 35, 259–275.

Connelly, V., Campbell, S., MacLean, M., and Barnes, J. (2006). Contribution of lower order skills to the written composition of college students with and without dyslexia. *Developmental Neuropsychology*, 29(1), 175–196.

Conners, F. A., Atwell, J. A., Rosenquist, C. J., and Sligh, A. C. (2001). Abilities underlying decoding differences in children with intellectual disability. *Journal of Intellectual Disability Research*, 45(4), 292–299.

Cooper, P. (2008). Like alligators bobbing for poodles? A critical discussion of education, ADHD and the biopsychosocial perspective. *Journal of Philosophy of Education*, 42(3–4), 457–474.

Cooper, P. (2011). Teacher strategies for effective intervention with students presenting social, emotional and behavioural difficulties: an international review. *European Journal of Special Needs Education*, 26(1), 71–86.

Coughlan, B., and Carpenter, B. (2013). Mental health and emotional wellbeing in students with disabilities: understanding the complexities involved. Paper presented at the Mental Health and Wellbeing for Children with Intellectual Disability Conference, Westpac Centre, Adelaide.

Covington, M. V. (2000). Goal theory, motivation, and school achievement: an integrative review. *Annual Review of Psychology*, 51(1), 171–200.

Davis, A. (2012). A monstrous regimen of synthetic phonics: fantasies of research-based teaching 'methods' versus real teaching. *Journal of Philosophy of Education*, 46(4), 560–573.

DCSF (2009a). *Lamb Inquiry: Special Educational Needs and Parental Confidence*. London: Department for Children, Schools and Families

DCSF (2009b). *School Workforce in England (including Local Authority level figures) January 2009 (Revised)*. London: Department for Children, Schools and Families.

Dehaene, S., and Cohen, L. (2011). The unique role of the visual word form area in reading. *Trends in Cognitive Science*, 15(6), 254–262.

DfE (2010). *The Importance of Teaching: The Schools White Paper 2010*. London: Department for Education.

DfE (2011). *Criteria for Assuring High-Quality Phonic Work*. London: Department for Education.

DfE (2012). *Increasing Opportunities for Young People and Helping Them to Achieve Their Potential*. London: Department for Education.

DfE (2013). *National Curriculum Assessments at Key Stage 2 in England, 2011/2012 (Revised)*. London: Department for Education.

DfE and DoH (2013a). *Draft Special Educational Needs (SEN) Code of Practice: For 0 to 25 Years*. London: Department for Education and Department of Health.

DfE and DoH (2013b). *Implementing the 0 to 25 Special Needs System. Government Advice for Local Authorities and Health Partners*. London: Department for Education and Department of Health.

DfEE (1998). *The National Literacy Strategy: Framework for Teaching*. London: Department for Education and Employment.

DfES (2001). *Special Educational Needs Code of Practice*. Nottingham: Department for Education and Skills.

DfES (2002). *Pupils, Teachers, Education Support Staff, Pupil: Teacher and Pupil: Adult Ratios in Maintained Schools in England: January 2002*. London: Department for Education and Skills.

DfES (2004). *Every Child Matters: Change for Children*. Nottingham: Department for Education and Skills.

DfES (2005a). *Assessment of Dyslexia, Dyspraxia, Dyscalculia and Attention Deficit Disorder (ADD) in Higher Education: Final Report of the SpLD Working Group*. London: Department for Education and Science.

DfES (2005b). *Learning Behaviour: The Report of the Practitioners' Group on School Behaviour and Discipline*. Nottingham: Department for Education and Skills.

DfES (2007). Social and emotional aspects of learning ... improving behaviour ... improving learning. Retrieved 1 September 2007, from http://www.standards.dfes.gov.uk/primary/publications/banda/seal/

Disability Rights UK (2014). *Into Higher Education 2014*. London: Disability Rights UK.

Driessen, G. (2007). The feminization of primary education: effects of teachers' sex on pupil achievement, attitudes and behaviour. *International Review of Education*, 53(2), 183–203.

Dweck, C. S. (2002). Caution: praise can be dangerous. In L. Abbeduto (ed.), *Taking Sides: Clashing Views on Controversial Issues in Educational Psychology* (pp. 117–125). Guildford: McGraw-Hill.

Dyslexia Research Institute (2014). The Dyslexia Research Institute Mission. Retrieved 21 January 2014, from http://www.dyslexia-add.org/

Edwards, J. (1994). *The Scars of Dyslexia*. London: Cassell.

Elik, N., Wiener, J., and Corkum, P. (2010). Pre-service teachers' open-minded thinking dispositions, readiness to learn, and attitudes about learning and behavioural difficulties in students. *European Journal of Teacher Education*, 33(2), 127–146.

Elliott, C. D. (2001). Cognitive profiles of poor readers. Paper presented at the Education Division of the British Psychological Society, Worcester.

Elliott, J. G. (2005). Dyslexia: diagnoses, debates and diatribes. *Special Children*, 169, 19–23.

Elliott, J. G., and Gibbs, S. (2008). Does dyslexia exist? *Journal of Philosophy of Education*, 42(3), 475–491.

Ellis, S., and Moss, G. (2013). Ethics, education policy and research: the phonics question reconsidered. *British Educational Research Journal*. doi: 10.1002/berj.3039

Emery, G. (1985). Principles of cognitive therapy. In A. T. Beck, G. Emery and R. Greenberg (eds), *Anxiety Disorders and Phobias: A Cognitive Perspective*. New York: Basic Books.

Epstein, R. M., Siegel, D. J., and Silberman, J. (2008). Self-monitoring in clinical practice: a challenge for medical educators. *Journal of Continuing Education in the Health Professions*, 28(1), 5–13.

Farrington-Flint, L. E., Coyne, J. S., and Heath., E. (2008). Variability in children's early reading strategies. *Educational Psychology*, 28(6), 649–661.

Faulkner, J., and Blyth, C. (1996). Dyslexia in higher education: an abuse of the system? *Educational Studies*, 22(3), 357–366.

Fawcett, A., and Nicholson, R. (1999). Performance of dyslexic children on cerebellar and cognitive tests. *Journal of Motor Behaviour*, 31(1), 68–78.

Fennell, M. (1999). *Overcoming Low Self-Esteem*. London: Constable and Robinson.

Fielding-Barnsley, R. (2010). Australian pre-service teachers' knowledge of phonemic awareness and phonics in the process of learning to read. *Australian Journal of Learning Difficulties*, 15(1), 99–110.

Fletcher, J. M. (2012). Classification and identification of learning disabilities. In B. Wong and D. L. Butler (eds), *Learning About Learning Disabilities* (4th edn, pp. 1–26). San Diego: Academic Press/Elsevier.

Forlin, C. (ed.). (2012). *Future Directions for Inclusive Teacher Education: An International Perspective*. London: Routledge.

Fox, L., Carta, J., Strain, P., Dunlap, G., and Hemmeter, M. L. (2009). *Response to Intervention and the Pyramid Model*. Florida: University of South Florida.

Fraser, J., Goswami, U., and Conti-Ramsden, G. (2010). Dyslexia and specific language impairment: the role of phonology and auditory processing. *Scientific Studies of Reading*, 14(1), 8–29.

Frederickson, N., and Cline, C. (2009). *Special Educational Needs, Inclusion and Diversity* (2nd edn). Maidenhead: Open University Press.

Fuchs, D., Mock, D., Morgan, P. L., and Young, C. L. (2003). Responsiveness-to-intervention: definitions, evidence, and implications for the learning disabilities construct. *Learning Disabilities Research and Practice*, 18(3), 157–171.

Fuchs, L. S., and Vaughn, S. (2012). Responsiveness-to-intervention a decade later. *Journal of Learning Disabilities*, 45(3), 195–203.

Gathercole, S. E., and Alloway, T. P. (2008). *Working Memory and Learning: A Practical Guide for Teachers*. London: Sage.

Gathercole, S. E., Willis, C. S., Baddeley, A. D., and Emslie, H. (1994). The children's test of nonword repetition: a test of phonological working memory. *Memory*, 2(2), 103–127.

Gersten, R., and Dimino, J. A. (2006). RTI (response to intervention): rethinking special education for students with reading difficulties (yet again). *Reading Research Quarterly*, 41(1), 99–108.

Gibbs, S. (2007). Teachers' perceptions of efficacy: beliefs that may support inclusion or segregation. *Educational and Child Psychology*, 24(3), 47–53.

Gibbs, S., and Powell, B. (2012). Teacher efficacy and pupil behaviour: the structure of teachers' individual and collective beliefs and their relationship with numbers of pupils excluded from school. *British Journal of Educational Psychology*, 82(4), 564–584.

Gilbert, J. K., Compton, D. L., Fuchs, D., Fuchs, L. S., Bouton, B., Barquero, L. A., and Cho, E. (2013). Efficacy of a first grade responsiveness-to-intervention prevention model for struggling readers. *Reading Research Quarterly*, 48(2), 135–154.

Goldacre, B. (2013). *Building Evidence into Education*. London: Department for Education.

Goodman, R. L., and Burton, D. M. (2010). The inclusion of students with BESD in mainstream schools: teachers' experiences of and recommendations for creating a successful inclusive environment. *Emotional and Behavioural Difficulties*, 15(3), 223–237.

Gornall, J. (2013). DSM: a fatal diagnosis? *British Medical Journal*, 346. doi: http://dx.doi.org/10.1136/bmj.f3256

Goswami, U. (2003). Why theories about developmental dyslexia require developmental designs. *Trends in Cognitive Science*, 7(12), 534–540.

Gough, P. B., and Tunmer, W. E. (1986). Decoding, reading, and reading disability. *Remedial and Special Education*, 7, 6–10.

Griffiths, Y., and Stuart, M. (2013). Reviewing evidence-based practice for pupils with dyslexia and literacy difficulties. *Journal of Research in Reading*, 36(1), 96–116.

Gwernan-Jones, R., and Burden, R. (2009). Are they just lazy? Student teachers' attitudes about dyslexia. *Dyslexia*, 16(1), 66–86.

Hallahan, D. P., Kauffman, J. M., and Pullen, P. C. (2012). *Exceptional Learners: An Introduction to Special Education* (12th edn). Upper Saddle River, NJ: Pearson Education.

Hallam, S., and Rogers, L. (2008). *Improving Behaviour and Attendance at School*. Maidenhead: Open University Press.

Hallett, F., and Armstrong, D. (2012). I want to stay over: a phenomenographic analysis of a short break/extended stay pilot project for children and young people with autism. *British Journal of Learning Disabilities*, 41(1), 66–72.

Hanbury, M. (2012). *Educating Students on the Autistic Spectrum: A Practical Guide* (2nd edn). London: Sage.

Hanley, T., Humphrey, N., and Lennie, C. (eds) (2012). *Adolescent Counselling Psychology: Theory, Research and Practice*. London: Routledge.

Harcourt Assessment (2005). *WIAT-IIUK Wechsler Individual Achievement Test. UK Scoring and Normative Supplement* (2nd edn). London: Harcourt Assessment.

Harden, A., Thomas, J., Scanlon, M., and Sinclair, J. (2003). *Supporting Pupils with Emotional and Behavioural Difficulties (EBD) in Mainstream Primary Schools: A Systematic Review of Recent Research on Strategy Effectiveness (1999 to 2002)*. London: EPPI-Centre, Social Science Research Unit, Institute of Education.

Hart, R. (2010). Classroom behaviour management: educational psychologists' views on effective practice. *Emotional and Behavioural Difficulties*, 15(4), 353–371.

Hatcher, J., Snowling, M. J., and Griffiths, Y. M. (2002). Cognitive assessment of dyslexic students in higher education. *British Journal of Educational Psychology*, 72, 119–133.

Hatcher, P. J., Hulme, C., Miles, J. N., Carroll, J. M., Hatcher, J., Gibbs, S., and Snowling, M. J. (2006). Efficacy of small group reading intervention for beginning readers with reading-delay: a randomised controlled trial. *Journal of Child Psychology and Psychiatry*, 47(8), 820–827.

Haugaard, J. J. (2008). *Child Psychopathology*. New York: McGraw-Hill.

Healey, J. J., Ahearn, W. H., Graff, R. B., and Libby, M. E. (2001). Extended analysis and treatment of self-injurious behaviour. *Behavioral Interventions*, 16, 181–195.

Heim, S., and Grande, M. (2012). Fingerprints of developmental dyslexia. *Trends in Neuroscience and Education*, 1, 10–14.

Heiman, T., and Kariv, D. (2004). Coping experience among students in higher education. *Educational Studies*, 30(4), 441–455.

HESA (2014). Tables from the students in higher education institutions publications. Retrieved 21 January 2014, from http://www.hesa.ac.uk/index.php/content/view/1973/239/

Hirvonen, R., Georgiou, G. K., Lerkkanen, M. K., Aunola, K., and Nurmi, J. E. (2010). Task-focused behaviour and literacy development: a reciprocal relationship. *Journal of Research in Reading*, 33(3), 302–319.

HMSO (1989). *The Elton Report. Discipline in Schools*. London: Her Majesty's Stationery Office.

HMSO (1995). *Disability Discrimination Act 1995*. London: Her Majesty's Stationery Office.

HMSO (2001). *Special Educational Needs and Disability Act 2001*. London: Her Majesty's Stationery Office.

HMSO (2010). *Equality Act 2010*. London: Her Majesty's Stationery Office.

Holloway, S. R., Náñez Sr, J. E., and Seitz, A. R. (2013). Word-Decoding as a Function of Temporal Processing in the Visual System. *PloS one*, 8(12), e84010.

Hoover, W. A., and Gough, P. B. (1990). The simple view of reading. *Reading and Writing: An Interdisciplinary Journal*, 2, 127–160.

Hornstra, L., Denessen, E., Bakker, J., van den Bergh, L., and Voeten, M. (2010). Teacher attitudes toward dyslexia: effects on teacher expectations and the academic achievement of students with dyslexia. *Journal of Learning Disabilities*, 43(6), 515–529.

Hruby, G. G. and Goswami, U. (2011). Neuroscience and reading: a review for reading education researchers. *Reading Research Quarterly*, 46(2), 156–172.

Huang, M. (2001). Cognitive abilities and the growth of high-IQ occupations. *Social Science Research*, 30, 529–551.

Hulme, C., and Snowling, M. J. (1994). *Reading Development and Dyslexia*. London: Whurr.

Hulme, C., and Snowling, M. J. (1997). *Dyselxia: Biology, Cognition and Intervention*. London: Whurr.

Hulme, C., and Snowling, M. J. (2013). Learning to read: what we know and what we need to understand better. *Child Development Perspectives*, 7, 1–5. doi: 10.1111/cdep.12005

Humphrey, N. (2004). The death of the feel good factors? Self-esteem in the educational context. *School Psychology International*, 24, 347–360.

Humphrey, N. (2012). Self-esteem in the classroom. In D. Armstrong and G. Squires (eds), *Contemporary Issues in Special Educational Needs: Considering the Whole Child* (pp. 74–84). Maidenhead: Open University Press/McGraw-Hill Education.

Humphrey, N., and Mullins, P. (2002). Personal constructs and attribution for academic success and failure in dyslexia. *British Journal of Special Education*, 29(4), 196–203.

Humphrey, N., and Squires, G. (2011). *DFE-RR176: Achievement for All: National Evaluation. Final Report*. London: Department for Education.

Humphrey, N., and Squires, G. (2012). Key note: the impact of Achievement for All (AfA) on outcomes for pupils with special educational needs in England: lessons for policy and practice. Paper presented at the National Council for Special Educational Needs Research Conference 2012, Croke Park Conference Centre, Dublin.

Iacoboni, M. (2009). Imitation, empathy, and mirror neurons. *Annual Review of Psychology*, 60, 653–670.

Ittenbach, R. F., Esters, I. G., and Wainer, H. (1997). The history of test development. In D. P. Flanagan, J. L. Genshaft and P. L. Harrison (eds), *Contemporary Intellectual Assessment: Theories, Tests, and Issues*. London: Guilford Press.

Jimerson, S. R., Burns, M. K., and VanDerHeyden, A. M. (eds) (2007). *Handbook of Response to Intervention: The Science and Practice of Assessment and Intervention*. New York: Springer.

Johnson, B., Freedman, L., and Rack, J. (2013). Dyslexia and summer-born children. *Dyslexia Review*, 24(3), 13–14.

Johnston, R. S., McGeown, S., and Watson, J. E. (2012). Long-term effects of synthetic versus analytic phonics teaching on the reading and spelling ability of 10 year old boys and girls. *Reading and Writing*, 25(6), 1365–1384.

Kendeou, P., Savage, R., and Broek, P. (2009). Revisiting the simple view of reading. *British Journal of Educational Psychology*, 79(2), 353–370.

Kirby, A., Sugden, D., Beveridge, S., Edwards, L., and Edwards, R. (2008a). Dyslexia and developmental co-ordination disorder in further and higher education: similarities and differences. Does the 'label' influence the support given? *Dyslexia*, 14, 197–213.

Kirby, A., Sugden, D., Beveridge, S., and Edwards, L. (2008b). Developmental co-ordination disorder (DCD) in adolescents and adults in further and higher education. *Journal of Research in Special Educational Needs*, 8(3), 120–131.

Klein, C. (1999). *Diagnosing Dyslexia: A Guide to the Assessment of Adults with Specific Learning Difficulties*. London: Basic Skills Agency.

Klotz, M. B., and Canter, A. (2007). *Response to Intervention (RTI): A Primer for Parents*. Bethesda, MD: National Association of School Psychologists.

Konur, O. (2002). Access to nursing education by disabled students: rights and duties of nursing programs. *Nurse Education Today*, 22, 364–374.

Lawrence, D. (1985). Improving self-esteem and reading. *Educational Research*, 27(3), 194–199.

Leggett, H., Sandars, J., and Burns, P. (2012). Helping students to improve their academic performance: a pilot study of a workbook with self-monitoring exercises. *Medical Teacher*, 34(9), 751–753.

Levy, F., Young, D. J., Bennett, K. S., Martin, N. C., and Hay, D. A. (2012). Comorbid ADHD and mental health disorders: are these children more likely to develop reading disorders? *ADHD Attention Deficit and Hyperactivity Disorders*, 5(1), 21–28.

Livingstone, M. S., and Hubel, D. H. (1987). Psychophysical evidence for separate channels for the perception of form, color, movement and depth. *Journal of Neuroscience*, 8, 4334–4339.

Lockley, S. (2002). Dyslexia and higher education: accessibility issues. *The Higher Education Academy*. Retrieved 6 April 2014, from http://www.engsc. ac.uk/assets/documents/resources/database/id416_dyslexia_and_higher_ education.pdf

Lovegrove, W. J., and Williams, M. C. (1993). Visual temporal processing deficits in specific reading disability. In D. Willows, R. S. Kruk and E. Corcos (eds), *Visual Processes in Reading and Reading Disabilities*. New Jersey: Lawrence Erlbaum Associates.

Lovitt, T. C. (2012). Applied behavior analysis: a method that languished but should be restored. *Intervention in School and Clinic*, 47(4), 252–256.

McDowell, M., and O'Keeffe, M. (2012). Public services for children with special needs: discrimination by diagnosis? *Journal of Paediatrics and Child Health*, 48(1), 2–5.

Mackay, N. (2006). *Removing Dyslexia as a Barrier to Achievement: The Dyslexia Friendly Schools Toolkit* (2nd edn). Wakefield: SEN Marketing.

Macleod, G. (2010). Identifying obstacles to a multidisciplinary understanding of 'disruptive' behaviour. *Emotional and Behavioural Difficulties*, 15(2), 95–109.

McLoughlin, D. (2012). Adults with dyslexia: reporting the findings from assessment. *Assessment and Development Matters*, 4(3), 33–35.

Mahar, N. E., and Richdale, A. L. (2008). Primary teachers' linguistic knowledge and perceptions of early literacy instruction. *Australian Journal of Learning Difficulties*, 13, 17–37.

Marsh, H. (1985). Self-concept: its multifaceted, hierarchical structure. *Educational Psychologist*, 20, 107–123.

Marshall, B. (2012). Synthetic phonics: the route to reading. In P. Adey and J. Dillon (eds), *Bad Education: Debunking Myths in Education*. New York: McGraw-Hill.

Martin, W., and Rezai-Rashti, G. (2009). Relationships between boys, teachers and education. In J. Budde and I. Mammes (eds), *Jungenforschung empirisch* (pp. 191–204). Weisbaden: VS Verlag für Sozialwissenschaften.

Matson, J. L., Bamburg, J. W., Cherry, K. E., and Paclawskyj, T. R. (1999). A validity study on the Questions About Behavioural Function (QABF) scale: predicting treatment success for self-injury, aggression, and stereotypies. *Research in Developmental Disabilities*, 20, 163–176.

MCEEDYA, Ministerial Council on Education, Early Childhood Development and Youth Affairs (2008). *The Melbourne Declaration on Educational Goals for Young Australians*. Retrieved 16 May 2014, from: https://www.education.gov.au/melbourne-declaration-educational-goals-young-people

Mesmer, H., and Griffith, P. (2005). Everybody's selling it: but just what is explicit, systematic phonics instruction? *The Reading Teacher*, 59(4), 366–376.

Miles, T. R. (1983). *Dyslexia: The Pattern of Difficulties*. London: Whurr.

Ministry of Education (2007). *The New Zealand Curriculum*. Wellington, New Zealand: Learning Media.

Ministry of Education, New Zealand (2013). *Special Education: Dyslexia, breaking down the barriers*. Retrieved 13 May 2014 from: http://www.minedu.govt.nz/Parents/AllAges/Usefullnformation/Dyslexia.aspx#HowWeAreHelping

Mooij, T., and Smeets, E. (2009). Towards systemic support of pupils with emotional and behavioural disorders. *International Journal of Inclusive Education*, 13(6), 597–616.

Moreno, G., and Bullock, L. M. (2011). Principles of positive behaviour supports: using the FBA as a problem-solving approach to address challenging behaviours beyond special populations. *Emotional and Behavioural Difficulties*, 16(2), 117–127.

Morgan, W. P. (1896). A case of congenital word blindness. *British Medical Journal*, 2(1871), 1378.

Morris, D. K., and Turnbull, P. A. (2007a). The disclosure of dyslexia in clinical practice: experiences of student nurses in the United Kingdom. *Nurse Education Today*, 27, 35–42.

Morris, D. K., and Turnbull, P. A. (2007b). A survey-based exploration of the impact of dyslexia on career progression of UK registered nurses. *Journal of Nursing Management*, 15, 97–106.

Morrow, L. M. (2005). *Literacy Development in the Early Years: Helping Children Read and Write*. Boston: Pearson/Allyn and Bacon.

Mowat, J. (2009). The inclusion of pupils perceived as having SEBD in mainstream schools: a focus upon learning. *Support for Learning*, 24(4), 159–169.

Mruk, C. J. (ed.). (1999). *Self-Esteem: Research, Theory and Practice* (2nd edn). New York: Springer.

Mullis, V. S., Martin, M. O., Foy, P., and Drucker, K. T. (2012). *PIRLS 2011 International Results in Reading*. Boston: International Association for the Evaluation of Educational Achievement (IEA).

National Institute of Child Health and Human Development and Early Child Care Research Network (2005). Pathways to reading: the role of oral language in the transition to reading. *Developmental Psychology*, 41(2), 428–442.

National Reading Panel (2000). *Teaching Children to Read: An Evidence-Based Assessment of the Scientific Research Literature on Reading and its Implications for Reading Instruction*. Washington, DC: National Institute of Child Health and Human Development.

NCSE (2011a). *Children with Special Educational Needs Information Booklet for Parents*. Dublin: National Council for Special Education.

NCSE (2011b). *Inclusive Education Framework: A Guide for Schools on the Inclusion of Pupils with Special Educational Needs*. Dublin: National Council for Special Education.

NEPS (2010). *A Continuum of Support for Post-Primary Schools*. Dublin: Department for Education and Skills.

New Mexico Education Department (2010). Conducting a functional behaviour assessment. New Mexico Public Education Department technical assistance manual. Retrieved 7th November 2013, from www.ped.state.nm.us/RtI/behavior/4.fba.11.28.pdf

Noble, T., and McGrath, H. (2008). The positive educational practices framework: a tool for facilitating the work of educational psychologists is promoting pupil wellbeing. *Educational and Child Psychology*, 25(2), 119–133.

Norgate, R. (1998). Reducing self-injurious behaviour in a child with severe learning difficulties: enhancing predictability and structure. *Educational Psychology in Practice*, 14, 176–182.

Nussbaum, M. C. (2011). *Creating Capabilities: The Human Development Approach*. Cambridge, MA: Harvard University Press.

OECD (2013). *Trends Shaping Education 2013*. Paris: OECD.

OFSTED (2005). *Managing Challenging Behaviour*. London: OFSTED.

OFSTED (2010). *The Special Educational Needs and Disability Review: A Statement is not Enough*. Manchester: OFSTED.

Olson, T. (1989). An architectural model of visual motion understanding. PhD thesis, University of Rochester.

O'Mara, A. J., Marsh, H. W., Craven, R. G., and Debus, R. L. (2006). Do self-concept interventions make a difference? A synergistic blend of construct validation and meta-analysis. *Educational Psychologist*, 41, 181–206.

O'Reilly, M. F. (1996). Assessment and treatment of episodic self-injury: a case study. *Research in Developmental Disabilities*, 17, 349–361.

Osmond, J. (1993). *The Reality of Dyslexia*. London: Cassell Educational.

Parkin, J. (2007). Stop feminising our schools: our boys are suffering. *Daily Mail*, 31 January.

PBS Parents (2014). The facts about dyslexia. Retrieved 21 January 2014, from http://www.pbs.org/parents/readinglanguage/articles/dyslexia/the_facts.html

Petley, J., Critcher, C., Hughes, J., and Rohloff, A. (eds) (2013). *Moral Panics in the Contemporary World*. London: A and C Black.

Pollo, T. C., Kessler, B., and Treiman, R. (2009). Statistical patterns in children's early writing. *Journal of Experimental Child Psychology*, 104, 410–426. doi: 10.1016/j.jecp.2009.07.003

Pollock, J., and Walker, E. (1994). *Day-to-Day Dyslexia in the Classroom*. London: Routledge.

Poulou, M., and Norwich, B. (2002). Cognitive, emotional and behavioural responses to students with emotional and behavioural difficulties: a model of decision-making. *British Educational Research Journal*, 28(1), 111–138.

Pumfrey, P. D. (2008). Moving towards inclusion? The first-degree results of students with and without disabilities in higher education in the UK: 1998–2005. *European Journal of Special Needs Education*, 23(1), 31–46.

Putwain, D., and Daniels, R. (2010). Is the relationship between competence beliefs and test anxiety influenced by goal orientation? *Learning and Individual Differences*, 20, 8–13.

Reid, G. (2012). *Dyslexia and Inclusion: Classroom Approaches for Assessment, Teaching and Learning*. London: Routledge.

Riddell, S., and Weedon, E. (2006). What counts as a reasonable adjustment? Dyslexic students and the concept of fair assessment. *International Studies in Sociology of Education*, 16(1), 57–73.

Riddell, S., Weedon, E., Fuller, M., Healey, M., Hurst, A., Kelly, K., and Piggott, L. (2007). Managerialism and equalities: tensions within widening access policy and practice for disabled students in UK universities. *Higher Education*, 54, 615–628.

Riddick, B. (1996). *Living With Dyslexia*. London: Routledge.

Riddick, B. (2001). Dyslexia and inclusion: time for a social model of disability perspective? *International Studies in Sociology of Education*, 11(3), 223–236.

Riddick, B. (2010). *Living with Dyslexia: The Social and Emotional Consequences of Specific Learning Difficulty* (2nd edn). London: Routledge.

Riddick, B. (2012). Labelling learners with SEND: the good, the bad and the ugly. In D. Armstrong and G. Squires (eds), *Contemporary Issues in Special Educational Needs: Considering the Whole Child* (pp. 25–34). Maidenhead: Open University Press/McGraw-Hill Education.

Riddick, B., Sterling, C., Farmer, M., and Morgan, S. (1999). Self-esteem and anxiety in the educational histories of adult dyslexic students. *Dyslexia*, 5, 227–248.

Ritzer, G. (2000). *Modern Sociological Theory*. Boston: McGraw-Hill.

Roane, H. S., Lerman, D. C., Kelley, M. E., and Van Camp, C. M. (1999). Within-session patterns of responding during functional analyses: the role of establishing operations in clarifying behavioural function. *Research in Developmental Disabilities*, 20, 73–89.

Roorda, D. L., Koomen, H., Spilt, J. L., and Oort, F. J. (2011). The influence of affective teacher-student relationships on students' school engagement and achievement: a meta-analytic approach. *Review of Educational Research*, 81(4), 493–529.

Rose, J. (2006). *Independent Review of the Teaching of Early Reading*. Nottingham: Department for Education and Skills.

Rose, J. (2009). *Identifying and Teaching Children and Young People with Dyslexia and Learning Difficulties*. London: Department for Children, Schools and Families.

Sanderson-Mann, J., and McCandless, F. (2005). Guidelines to the United Kingdom Disability Discrimination Act (DDA) 1995 and the Special Educational Needs and Disability Act (SENDA) 2001with regard to nurse education and dyslexia. *Nurse Education Today*, 25, 542–549.

Shapiro, L. R., and Solity, J. E. (2008). Delivering phonological and phonics training within whole-class teaching. *British Journal of Educational Psychology*, 78(4), 597–620.

Shapiro, L. R., Carroll, J. M., and Solity, J. E. (2013). Separating the influences of prereading skills on early word and nonword reading. *Journal of Experimental Child Psychology*, 116(2), 278–295.

Share, D. (1995). Phonological recoding and self-teaching: sine qua non of reading acquisition. *Cognition*, 55, 151–208.

Shovman, M. M., and Ahissar, M. (2006). Isolating the impact of visual perception on dyslexics' reading ability. *Vision Research*, 46(20), 3514–3525. doi: http://dx.doi.org/10.1016/j.visres.2006.05.011

Slaghuis, W., and Lovegrove, W. J. (1985). Spatial frequency mediated visible persistence and specific reading disability. *Brain and Cognition*, 4, 219–240.

Sniehotta, F. F. (2009). Towards a theory of intentional behaviour change: plans, planning, and self-regulation. *British Journal of Health Psychology*, 14(2), 261–273.

Snowling, M. J. (1981). Phonemic deficits in developmental dyslexia. *Psychological Research*, 43, 219–234.

Snowling, M. J. (2013). Early identification and interventions for dyslexia: a contemporary view. *Journal of Research for Special Educational Needs*, 13(1), 7–14.

Snowling, M. J., and Hulme, C. (2011). Evidence-based interventions for reading and language difficulties: creating a virtuous circle. *British Journal of Educational Psychology*, 81(1), 1–23.

Snowling, M. J., Hulme, C., and Nation, K. (1997). A connectionist perspective on the development of reading skills in chidlren. *Trends in Cognitive Science*, 1, 88–91.

Snowling, M. J., Bishop, D. V. M., and Stothard, S. E. (2000). Is pre-school language impairment a risk factor for dyslexia in adolescence? *Journal of Child Psychology and Psychiatry*, 41, 587–600.

Snowling, M. J., Muter, V., and Carroll, J. M. (2007). Children at family risk of dyslexia: a follow-up in early adolescence. *Journal of Child Psychology and Psychiatry*, 48(6), 609–618.

Soles, T., Bloom, E. L., Heath, N. L., and Karagiannakis, A. (2008). An exploration of teachers' current perceptions of children with emotional and behavioural difficulties. *Emotional and Behavioural Difficulties*, 13(4), 275–290.

Soltani, A., and Roslan, S. (2013). Contributions of phonological awareness, phonological short-term memory, and rapid automated naming, toward decoding ability in students with mild intellectual disability. *Research in Developmental Disabilities*, 34(3), 1090–1099.

South Australian Government (2013). Intellectual disability. Retrieved 6 April 2014, from http://www.sa.gov.au/topics/community-support/disability/disability-types/intellectual-disability

SpLD Assessment Standards Committee (2010). Updated guidance re. BAS and WISC. Retrieved 1 July 2011, from http://www.sasc.org.uk/ per cent28S per cent28ybkovhztjga40545wyg5y1zs per cent29 per cent29/Default.aspx?id=2

SpLD Test Evaluation Committee (2009). *Suitable Tests for the Assessment of Specific Learning Difficulties in Higher Education (Revised October 2009)*. London: Department for Education and Science.

Squires, G. (2001). Dyslexia friendly. *Special Children*, 142, 24–27.

Squires, G. (2002). Classroom strategies to support dyslexic children in mainstream classrooms. SEN Newsletter (Spring). Staffordshire County Council.

Squires, G. (2003). Cognitive preference and spelling difficulties. Doctorate in Educational Psychology thesis, University of Manchester.

Squires, G. (2004). Supporting children with …. *Special Children*, 158, 21–29.

Squires, G. (2010). Analysis of local authority data to show the impact of being dyslexia friendly on school performance. *Staffordshire Schools Governors Newsletter*, Autumn 2010, 9.

Squires, G. (2012). Historical and socio-political agendas around defining and including children with special educational needs. In D. Armstrong and G. Squires (eds), *Contemporary Issues in Special Educational Needs: Considering the Whole Child* (pp. 9–24). Maidenhead: Open University/McGraw-Hill Education.

Squires, G., and McKeown, S. (2003). *Supporting Children with Dyslexia*. Birmingham: Questions.

Squires, G., and McKeown, S. (2006). *Supporting Children with Dyslexia* (2nd edn). New York: Continuum.

Squires, G., Humphrey, N., and Barlow, A. (2013). Over-identification of special educational needs in younger members of the age cohort: differential effects of level of assessment and category of need. *Assessment and Development Matters*, 5(1), 23–26.

Squires, G., Humphrey, N., Barlow, A., and Wigelsworth, M. (2012). The identification of Special Educational Needs and the month of birth: differential effects of category of need and level of assessment. *European Journal of Special Needs Education*, 27(4), 469–481. doi: 10.1080/08856257.2012.711961

Stainthorp, R., and Stuart, M. (2008). The simple view of reading and evidence-based practice. Retrieved 9 September 2013, from www.ucet.ac.uk/downloads/1511

Stanovich, K. E. (1986). Matthew effects in reading: some consequences of individual differences in the acquisition of literacy. *Reading Research Quarterly*, 21, 360–406.

Stanovich, K. E. (2000). *Progress in Understanding Reading: Scientific Foundations and New Frontiers*. London: Guilford Press.

Steer, A. (2009). *Learning Behaviour: Lessons learned. A Review of Behaviour Standards and Practices in our Schools*. London: Department for Children, Schools and Families.

Stein, J. (1994). A visual defect in dyslexics? In A. Fawcett and R. Nicholson (eds), *Dyslexia in Children: Multidisciplinary Perspectives*. Hemel Hempstead: Harvester Wheatsheaf.

Stein, J. (1996). Visual systems and reading. In C. H. Chase, G. D. Rosen and G. F. Sherman (eds), *Developmental Dyslexia: Neural, Cognitive and Genetic Mechanisms*. Maryland: York Press.

Stein, J., and Fowler, S. (1985). Effect of monocular occlusion on visuomotor perception and reading in dyslexic children. *The Lancet*, 326(8446), 69–73. doi: http://dx.doi.org/10.1016/S0140-6736(85)90179-5

Sternberg, R. J., and Kaufman, S. B. (2012). Trends in intelligence research. *Intelligence*, 40, 2, 235–236.

Strand, S. (2006). Comparing the predictive validity of reasoning tests and national end of Key Stage 2 tests: which tests are the 'best'? *British Educational Research Journal*, 32, 209–225.

Stuart, M., Stainthorp, R., and Snowling, M. J. (2008). Literacy as a complex activity: deconstructing the simple view of reading. *Literacy*, 42, 59–66.

Talcott, J. B., Hansen, P. C., Willis-Owen, C., McKinnell, I. W., Richardson, A. J., and Stein, J. (1998). Visual magnocellular impairment in adult developmental dyslexics. *Neuro-Ophthalmology*, 20, 187–201.

Thorndike, R. M. (1997). The early history of intelligence testing. In D. P. Flanagan, J. L. Genshaft and P. L. Harrison (eds), *Contemporary Intellectual Assessment: Theories, Tests, and Issues*. London: Guilford Press.

Tincani, M. J., Castrogiavanni, A., and Axelrod, S. (1999). A comparison of the effectiveness of brief versus traditional functional analysis. *Research in Developmental Disabilities*, 20, 327–338.

Treiman, R. (1997). Spelling in normal children and dyslexics. In B. A. Blachman (ed.), *Foundations of Reading Acquisition and Dyslexia: Implications for Early Intervention* (pp. 191–218). Hillsdale, NJ: Erlbaum.

Tschannen-Moran, M., and Woolfolk Hoy, A. (2007). The differential antecedents of self-efficacy beliefs of novice and experienced teachers. *Teaching and Teacher Education*, 23(6), 944–956.

UNESCO (1994a). *Final Report: World Conference on Special Needs Education: Access and Quality*. Paris: UNESCO.

UNESCO (1994b). *The Salamanca Statement and Framework for Action on Special Needs Education*. Salamanca, Spain: UNESCO.

UNESCO (2000). *The Dakar Framework for Action. Education for All: Meeting our Collective Commitments*. Paris: UNESCO.

United Nations (2006). Convention on the rights of people with disabilities. Retrieved 22 February 2014, from http://www.un.org/disabilities/convention/conventionfull.shtml

US Department of Education (2004). Individuals with Disabilities Education Act of 2004. Retrieved 27 November 2013, from http://idea.ed.gov/download/finalregulations.html

US Department of Education, US(2009). *Building the Legacy: IDEA 2004*. Retrieved 13 May 2014, from: http://idea.ed.gov/

Vaughn, S., and Fletcher, J. M. (2012). Response to intervention with secondary school students with reading difficulties. *Journal of Learning Disabilities*, 45(3), 244–256.

Vellutino, F. R., Fletcher, J. M., Snowling, M. J., and Scanlon, D. M. (2004). Specific reading disability (dyslexia): what have we learned in the past four decades? *Journal of Child Psychology and Psychiatry*, 45, 2–40.

Vickermana, P., and Blundell, M. (2010). Hearing the voices of disabled students in higher education. *Disability and Society*, 25(1), 21–32.

Vollmer, T. R., and Smith, R. G. (1996). Some current themes in functional analysis research. *Research in Developmental Disabilities*, 17, 229–249.

von der Embse, N., Barterian, J., and Segool, N. (2013). Test anxiety interventions for children and adolescents: a systematic review of treatment studies from 2000–2010. *Psychology in the Schools*, 50(1), 57–71.

Wang, S., and Gathercole, S. E. (2013). Working memory deficits in children with reading difficulties: memory span and dual task coordination. *Journal of Experimental Child Psychology*, 115(1), 118–197.

Watts, Z., and Gardner, P. (2013). Is systematic synthetic phonics enough? Examining the benefit of intensive teaching of high frequency words (HFW) in a year one class. *Education 3–13*, 41(1), 100–109.

Wearmouth, J., Soler, J., and Reid, G. (2003). *Meeting Difficulties in Literacy Development: Research, Policy and Practice*. London: Psychology Press.

Webster, R., Blatchford, P., Bassett, P., Brown, P., Martin, C., and Russell, A. (2010). Double standards and first principles: framing teaching assistant support for pupils with special educational needs. *European Journal of Special Educational Needs*, 25(4), 319–336.

Wechsler, D. (2004). *WISC-IV: Technical and Interpretative Manual*. San Antonio: Harcourt Assessment.

Wyse, D., and Styles, M. (2007). Synthetic phonics and the teaching of reading: the debate surrounding England's 'Rose report'. *Literacy*, 41(1), 35–42.

Yamamoto, H., Kita, Y., Kobayashi, T., Yamazaki, H., Kaga, M., Hoshino, H., and Inagaki, M. (2013). Deficits in Magnocellular Pathway in Developmental Dyslexia: A Functional Magnetic Resonance Imaging-Electroencephalography Study. *Journal of Behavioral and Brain Science*, 3, 168–178.

Yin, R. K. (2014). *Case Study Research: Design and Methods* (6th edn). London: Sage.

Zimmerman, B. J., and Schunk, D. H. (eds) (2013). *Self-Regulated Learning and Academic Achievement: Theoretical Perspectives*. London: Routledge.

Index